HAUNTED BALDWIN COUNTY, ALABAMA

HAUNTED BALDWIN COUNTY, ALABAMA

HARRIET BRILL OUTLAW

IMAGES BY PENNY H. TAYLOR

Haunted America

Published by Haunted America
A Division of The History Press
Charleston, SC 29403
www.historypress.net

Cover images: Front photo by author. Back photo by Penny H. Taylor.
Opposite: The home of the author.

Photos by Penny H. Taylor unless otherwise noted.

First published 2015

Manufactured in the United States

ISBN 978.1.62619.874.6

Library of Congress Control Number: 2015941005

Notice: The information in this book is true and complete to the best of our knowledge. It is offered without guarantee on the part of the author or The History Press. The author and The History Press disclaim all liability in connection with the use of this book.

*This book is dedicated to Benulee, my home, which has a spirit of its own—
a legacy that anchors everything in place.*

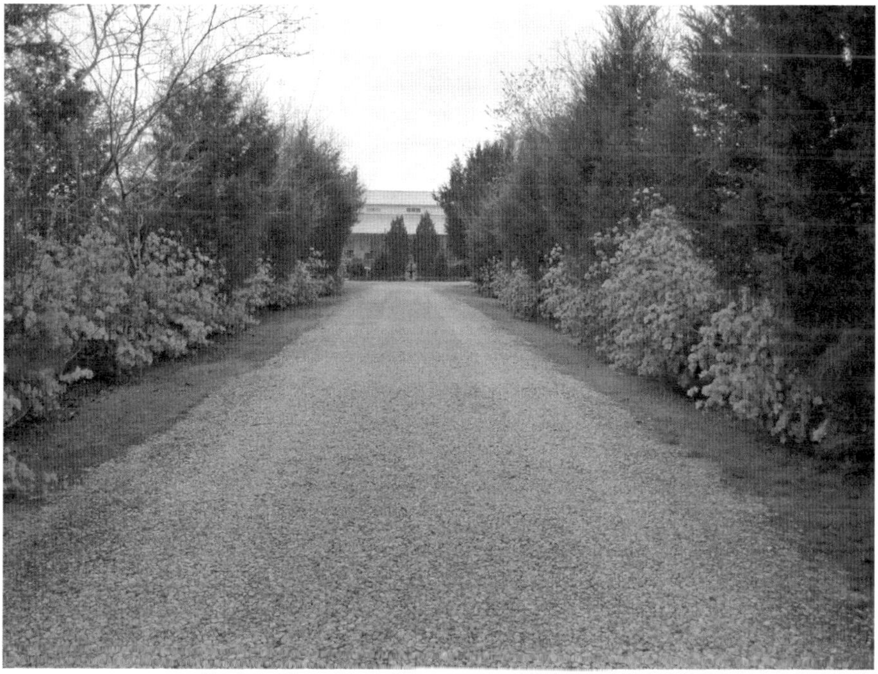

Come, sit on my porch and let's tell stories.

CONTENTS

FOREWORD

A crop of stories is ready for harvest from storytelling seeds planted across the southern region of America and beyond by Alabama's nationally known storyteller and author Kathryn Tucker Windham. Windham's soulful voice and captivating stories touched, and continue to touch, the hearts and minds of listeners and readers of all ages. *Alabama's One Big Front Porch*, *Thirteen Alabama Ghosts and Jeffrey* and other works written by Kathryn Tucker Windham have inspired listeners and readers to become tellers and writers, too. Harriet Outlaw was inspired. *Haunted Baldwin County, Alabama* is Outlaw's tribute to Kathryn Tucker Windham's legacy to storytelling.

"Thank you most for fanning the flame of storytelling…Generations to come will thank you."

–Kathryn Tucker Windham
February 23, 2010

DEBORAH RANKINS TUNSTALL
Kathryn Tucker Windham Library and Museum
Alabama Southern Community College
and
the Alabama Folklife Association Board of Directors

Preface

Do I believe in ghosts? Join the crowd in asking me that question. I'll answer that with another question: "Do you?"

I certainly believe that feelings and energies can be transported through space and time. I grew up hearing wonderful stories told at night on our front porch in the glory days before television, the Internet and video games—when the human voice created the bonds between friends, family and, especially, the past. My love for stories, true and sometimes enhanced, led me to a lifetime of treasuring folklore. I am a storyteller and make no apology for the tale-telling flavor of these episodes. They relate the stories I have been told for more than fifty years, and I believe each one of them. I know that something does not have to be proven true to be believed. Some truths just can't be proven. So, yes, I do believe. I believe that the "haint" blue paint on the ceilings of southern porches deters evil from coming into the house. I believe that the wind whistling through the mouths of the blue bottles on the bottle tree in the yard warns all unhappiness to stay away. And, yes, I believe that sounds and sights from the past can be detected by those here in this plane who look and listen.

I believe that those sights and sounds experienced here in this world that we call "hauntings" are not only unfinished dreams of those spirits not free to "pass over" but also those that are free to come and go—those who felt such joy in this life that they had heaven on earth and are still experiencing this earthly place as a part of their paradise. And I believe in the communion of saints.

I am not interested in imaginary horror stories or unexplained sounds or apparitions. I want to know the why, who and how of the real story. Or at least the real story that I believe—those stories that the old folks still tell on the front porch. When you get down to it, a person's belief trumps the truth every time. I believe there is always a story behind the haunting. I know that the blue paint and the bottle tree assure me that only those stories are allowed on our porch. So come sit on my porch, and let's tell those stories.

Acknowledgements

When a project like this begins, the author has no idea what will emerge when word gets around that experiences are being collected. I have been delighted to find so many people willing to share their stories and resources. There is no way I can name every person who has helped me, but there are a few who have just been amazing. First, my dear friend and colleague Penny Taylor and her husband, Ken Balme, have spent countless hours traveling the county, interviewing and photographing those nooks and crannies in all corners. Special thanks to Sherri, Barbara and Karen, who have taught me so much about seeking out the paranormal. I have deep respect for those serious investigators and do not claim to be as knowledgeable as many of them are.

Donnie Barrett of the Fairhope City Museum is a walking encyclopedia and knows everybody who knows anything! Author Joan Crowder, as seen in her book *Tell It to an Old Hollow Log*, is an incredible local authority who is most willing to share. Grand Hotel specialists Susan Stein and Bob Glennon have been most supportive, and I greatly appreciate the contributions made by Robert Normand, the son of the great bandleader Jack Normand. Fort Mims advocate Claudia Slaughter and the Morris family welcomed us to the northern realms of the county and more than willingly shared their experiences with us. The Baldwin County Historical Commission deserves recognition for the work it does preserving local historical sites, especially the Swift-Coles Historic Home in Bon Secour. Thanks go to the commission and Historic Home Director Sandra Forsman. Gulf Shores Park ranger

Dave Baumhauer helped us find the real Catman Trail, and Mike Bailey opened my eyes to sights unseen at Fort Morgan. Rob Woodruff snapped a wonderful photo of a Frenchman in the D'Olive Cemetery, and Elizabeth Parker, author of *Haunted Mobile*, manages a fabulous blog where loads of stories are posted. The Foley Railroad Museum and the Foley Library are amazing repositories of all things Baldwin, and thanks go to Directors Bonnie Donaldson, John Jackson and Jeannette Bornholdt, who have such a clear vision of preservation. A special note of appreciation also goes to all of those resources who wish to remain anonymous. Thank you.

Everyone who attempts to write the tales of hauntings in Alabama pays tribute to Kathryn Tucker Windham, who inspired and encouraged me. I appreciate the foreword by Deborah Rankins Tunstall, who performs an outstanding service as director of the Kathryn Tucker Windham Museum in Monroeville, Alabama. And of course, I must tell my husband how deeply I love him and appreciate his willingness to be a part of this and all of my other crazy schemes. He declares that if there are any mistakes in this work, I say he is to blame. What do you think?

INTRODUCTION

MY VERY OWN GHOST

I always told my children and grandchildren that there is no ghost in our home, but it is time for me to break the silence and come clean. Miss Abbie is here just as surely as we are. We live in a reproduction home, an exact replica of the home in which I was born and reared in Mobile, Alabama. The house has a spirit of its own and is also home to an apparition that keeps me company with the past.

The original house was built in 1835 as a simple dogtrot-style country home on the banks of Three Mile Creek, just north of downtown Mobile. Soon the dogtrot was enclosed and a second story added to house the large family who lived there. The house had two main rooms on each side of the central passageway, as well as large front and rear porches. It originally faced the creek, but in the 1920s, the Fowler family remodeled it to face Pleasant Avenue. They added stucco to the front porch as well as the inside walls. Then the Depression hit, and the Fowlers had to sell the house.

That is when my parents, Oscar and Harriet Brill, entered the picture. Actually, my father's family had lived in the house when he was a child, and he had always dreamed of returning to live in that wonderful house. He and my mother had married in 1930 and were soon running a little mom and pop store, the Hill Top, on Costarides Street in Toulminville, a short distance from the "Big House." They were living in a house connected to the Hill Top Grocery and raising four children when the Big House came up for purchase. Their hard work at the store, my dad's full-time job at Mobile Paint Company and a cottage industry repairing bedsprings had enabled them to save a little money. For a family during the Depression, the purchase of a house was a daunting prospect, but they stepped out on faith. Using their nest egg, they bid for the house and purchased it, loaded their truck and moved into the house, which immediately became a real home in every sense of the word.

At the time they moved in, there were few other homes in the neighborhood, but soon World War II workers were looking for homes and small rental places sprang up all around. Bragg Hill Apartments were built to the west of the house, on the corner of Stanton Road and Pleasant Avenue, in 1947. They were built on the estate of the Bragg Mitchell Mansion, which still stands across the creek on Springhill Avenue and is home to many ghosts, as related by Elizabeth Parker in *Haunted Mobile*.

There was another antebellum house east of our Big House, just across the sunken roadbed of the ancient Rondo Road (formerly Center Street), which originally crossed Three Mile Creek. That home was a real southern mansion, built by a highly respected Mobile family in the early 1800s. It was one of those magnificent structures that had porches upstairs and downstairs, a cellar and several outbuildings. My mother became very good friends with the last member of the family to live in the house, Miss Abbie. They often visited over cups of tea in her parlor. Abbie was indeed a genteel and fine southern lady who spent her life teaching piano lessons, caring for the family home and carrying on a legacy of southern culture.

Miss Abbie loved her home just as my mother loved ours. They were bonded by the love each had for her home—not merely dwellings of sticks and bricks but treasure boxes holding the memories of the days past and the promise of days to come, the tangible cornerstones of everything else in life. These sister houses were two of the few houses that can claim ownership of a soul, for souls they did indeed possess.

As the ladies shared many a story throughout the years, they often told of the presence of mysterious sightings and sounds. Miss Abbie told my mother the story of her ancestor, the Mistress of the House in the 1860s. When the Confederate forces were constructing earthwork mounds and batteries along the banks of Three Mile Creek, they were thwarted in cutting down a one-hundred-year-old live oak tree as the lady stood in front of the tree. The tree stood there until the hurricane of 1916 split it down the center and it thundered to the ground. The corpse of that grand tree lay there as a tribute to the beauty of nature. During the Depression, people were allowed to come and cut branches to use for firewood. Many people told of seeing the lady in white standing in front of the tree. There were many neighborhood

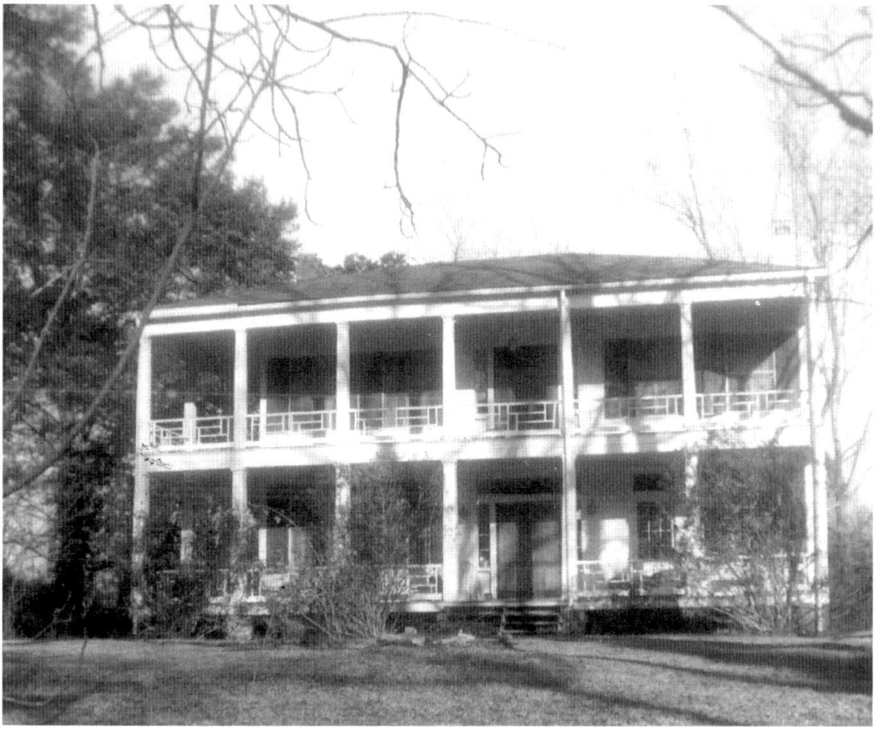

Miss Abbie's plantation home in Toulminville, Alabama, on Three Mile Creek. *Author's collection.*

stories of soldiers on horses riding in the waters of the creek, and sometimes people claimed to see a crippled man in a Confederate uniform in the yard of the antebellum home.

My mother had mysterious stories to share about our home as well. The Fowler family had told her that they had found a pair of alabaster vases and a large brass key in the attic. They put them on the mantel in the parlor, but when they returned home one day after church, the vases were shattered on the floor and the key was missing. We often heard the cries of an infant that seemed to come from the crawl space between the first and second floors. I grew up hearing these stories and honoring the heritage of the two houses.

Of noted interest were the painted window shades that hung in the parlor of Miss Abbie's house. The canvas shades had been painted in the 1830s and were protected for more than one hundred years by the outside shutters that Miss Abbie kept closed year round. Miss Abbie was homebound in her later years and moved to a nursing home soon after I was born in 1947.

She died two years later. After Miss Abbie's death, my mother purchased seven of those shades and put them in our home, where they stayed until my mother sold our home in 1970. They hang today in the reproduction house we built so that the shades could once again have a home. In fact, this house is actually here so that Miss Abbie and my mother can return home as well.

Other families who lived in Miss Abbie's house through the years told of presences there, but none was frightening. The final owner of the home determined that it had served its purpose and scheduled demolition of the house in 1965. Our family mourned the demise of the house but tried to accept the adage that houses are really built for people, not people for houses. Or is that really true when a house has a soul?

We watched the process of the house coming down and saved some of the wooden pegs that held the foot-wide joists in place for more than 130 years. I distinctly remember that the last part of the house to remain in place was the center wall, which supported the massive staircase to the second floor. As I stood at the eastward window in our living room looking across the ancient roadbed, I saw the wall come down. I screamed for my mother. The wall had clearly fallen on someone who was standing next to it and looking directly into my eyes. I can remember those sad eyes. My mother and I hurried to the site and told the foreman that I had seen the wall fall on someone. As you would expect, when they searched there was no one there.

I was a student commuting to the University of South Alabama in the fall of that year. I returned home one evening at about ten o'clock and turned in the dirt lane. I noticed a figure in the front yard. It was clearly a lady dressed in black, with a white dust cap on her head. She was bent almost double and was leaning on a wooden walking stick that I could clearly see. I turned the car to shine the lights on her, and I could see her even more distinctly. The closer I drove toward her, the more transparent she became, and by the time I was within fifteen feet, she had completely disappeared. I was not afraid. I instinctively knew that this was Miss Abbie, homeless. I spoke to her, inviting her to come into our home that evening. I woke up my parents to relay the experience, but they were not alarmed either. In fact, they seemed relieved to know that Miss Abbie had come to live with us. I asked my mother why she thought I was the one able to see the apparition, and she told me that Miss Abbie had loved me so very much and must have known that I would take care of her as long as I lived. A most interesting fact is that I had no memory of seeing Miss Abbie in her later years, and no one had ever told me that Miss Abbie was bent double in her old age—that is why she walked with a cane.

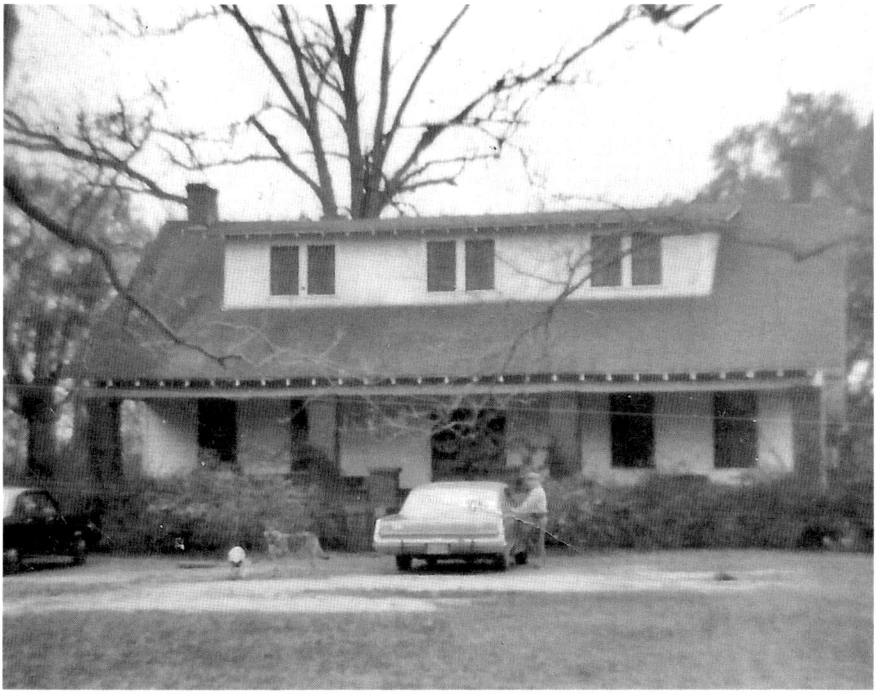

Author's original home in Toulminville, Alabama, built circa 1835. Miss Abbie appeared in a sketch made from the photograph pictured here. *Author's collection.*

That Christmas, as a gift to my parents, I had taken a photo of the house and had an artist sketch it in pencil. Of course, the artist, Rob Bearden, had no knowledge of Miss Abbie, and yet she is clearly visible in the upstairs window of my bedroom in the sketch.

My mother sold the house, and when it was demolished in 1978, we did not know ahead of time and were unable to secure any original architectural elements. However, we were able to retrieve Miss Abbie, but not until 1993! My husband and I decided to build a replica of my homeplace for my mother in her last years and chose a lovely pecan orchard in Fairhope, just like the pecan orchard of the original house. As we reproduced the Big House, we knew that this house would be as special as the original. The measurements are all the same—the windows, doors, creaks and cracks have all taken on the spirit of the old place. This structure has a soul because of the memories it keeps alive, but it gets better. After we had moved into our new home, I took a little visit to the old homeplace. You know what happened, don't you? I invited Miss Abbie to come home with me and live in our new home.

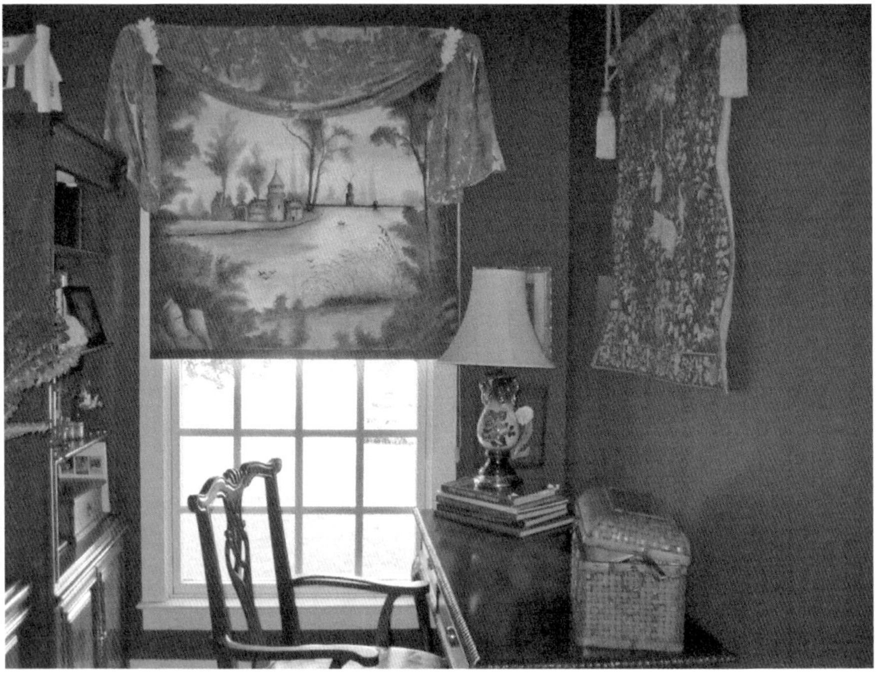

The corner of author's home that is the favorite spot for Miss Abbie to make herself known.

I know that she did. I feel her especially in the corner of our living room, the replica of the one that once had the clearest view of her homeplace. After we first moved in, that corner was a headache. The rain that leaked in could not be stopped. The drapes on that window were often askew, and the painted window shade was at different heights at different times.

One day, while I was studying photos of the original house, I realized that corner window had always been the location of a window shade that had a painted castle on it. That particular window shade had been given to a grandson by my mother, so it was not among those that hung in our new home. I knew then what was distressing Miss Abbie. I went to the corner with the photo and explained to her that the window shade was loved and well preserved, but not in this house. From that moment on, the rain did not leak in, the curtains and shade stayed in place and I felt a great sense of peace there. She is here with me at my writing desk, with her precious window shades hanging once again. I love hearing her walking cane thumping on the hard pine floors, and sometimes I see her shadow sitting in the parlor with a cup of tea. I sit and remember with her.

PART I
NORTH BALDWIN COUNTY

Baldwin County is one of the largest counties in the United States, spanning more than one hundred miles from the shores of the Gulf of Mexico to its northernmost reaches. Most early settlers came to North Baldwin, the Tensaw Community, home of the Muskogean Creek nation, and established large farms on the banks of the navigable rivers. This area was part of the Mississippi Territory when Baldwin County was created in 1809, before there was even a state of Alabama. As a part of the Mobile Delta, the terrain is mystical and has deep secrets and unexplained mysteries. These are the stuff from which the hauntings of the area are made and passed down for generations. Come sit on the porch. Let's tell stories.

THIEF IN THE CHURCH ATTIC: MONTGOMERY HILL BAPTIST CHURCH

Old folks at Montgomery Hill Baptist Church in Tensaw reminisce about the days when their grandparents discovered that a convict had been hiding out in the attic of their church for several months. During the late eighteenth century, the area in North Baldwin was the most populated part of the county, as it was a part of the Mississippi Territory and many Americans built homes and farms along the river. It was here that the Montgomery Hill Baptist Church was built in 1854 by those early families, some of whom, no doubt, had heard sermons delivered by the famous traveling evangelist Lorenzo Dow when he came through the area. The congregation, which was officially formed in 1840, raised more than $1,400 to build the Greek Revival–style church, constructed using wooden pegs rather than nails. The church remains the oldest standing active church in Baldwin County; the slave gallery, original lighting, interior graining and pine pews are still in use today. The graveyard tombstones bear the names of some of the earliest families: Earle, Tate, Mims, Bryant, Holmes and Smith.

The story of the moving of the court records from Daphne to Bay Minette has been told so many times that the facts are still in dispute. Daphne was reluctant to relinquish the county seat, so citizens of Bay Minette took wagons to Daphne and loaded up the records, the furniture and even the jail fixtures. A story goes that one of the inmates in the jail helped disassemble the cell and load it onto one of the wagons. Upon his arrival in Bay Minette, he helped install the fixtures and then was once again locked inside. A new jail was built in 1910, and this time he made an escape during his transfer. He eluded capture, but as no one seemed to know why he was even imprisoned, the manhunt was not very extensive.

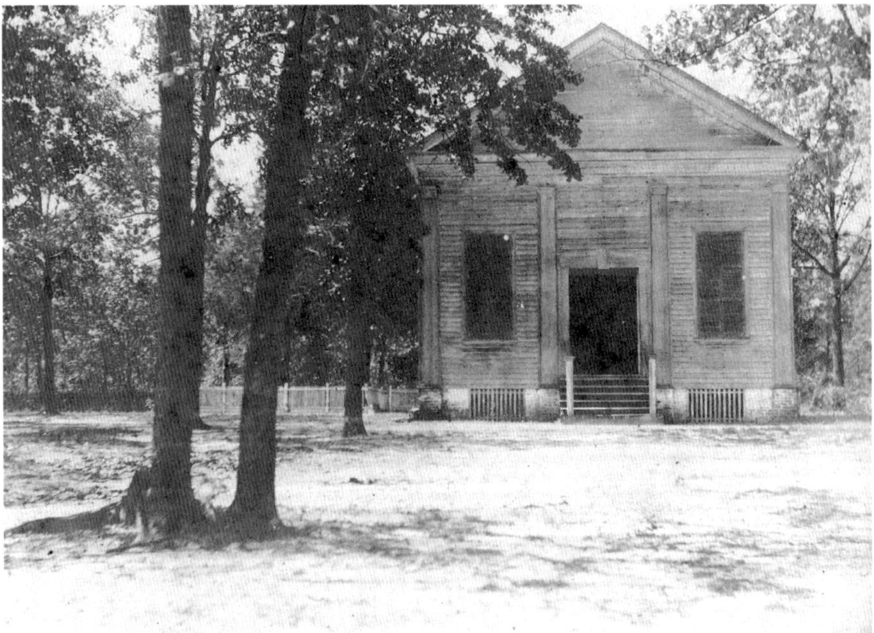

Montgomery Hill Baptist Church, Tensaw, Alabama. *Author's collection.*

Soon after his escape, people living within five miles of Montgomery Hill Church began noticing that an occasional ham or slab of bacon went missing from a smokehouse or that chickens disappeared from henhouses, but most thought that wild animals had just come in and helped themselves to dinner. Bears, foxes and panthers (or "painters") were common in those days up in Tensaw country.

After a while, at dinner on the grounds, members began to compare their losses and realized that this rash of disappearing foodstuff was just too much to be natural coincidences—someone was actually stealing from them. Soon after, one local saw a man leaving his henhouse with a chicken clutched under his arm and followed the thief until he lost him in the woods. The local contacted the sheriff in Bay Minette, who came to the house with his hunting dogs. They followed the trail nearly to the church but lost it. They were determined to find this thief, so they set a trap. They waited in the woods the next night, and when a man left the church, they followed him to a nearby farm, where they witnessed him raiding the smokehouse. There they arrested him. The sheriff recognized him as the missing inmate, took him to the Bay Minette jail and locked him up again. Upon investigating the church attic, they found that he had been there quite a while. They saw bedding of corn shucks and a stack of chicken and ham bones in the corner.

The well-fed convict was remorseful and even quite calm as they took him back to jail. It was not long before he was preaching to his fellow inmates and telling them of the ways he had heard about during the church services. You see, he could hear the preachers and the testimonies of the congregation, and he found a new way of life. Parishioners heard about his conversion, and members of the church posted his bail, refusing to press charges. He returned to Tensaw, where he lived the rest of his life, tending the church grounds and taking special pains to ensure the maintenance of the cemetery.

No one has been able to find a record of his burial, but some say that he was quietly laid to rest in an unmarked grave in the cemetery he loved. Many visitors to the cemetery at night tell of hearing a voice that sounds like a preacher delivering a hellfire and brimstone sermon, even though the words are indistinguishable. Some say they can hear the word *repent* spoken again and again. One local resident said that she has often gone to the cemetery at night but feels an eerie presence and does not even get out of her vehicle. Teens, daring one another to persevere overnight in the cemetery, have said that a shadowy figure can be seen walking among the tombstones. Most indicative of the thief's presence is the fact that nearly every time the church

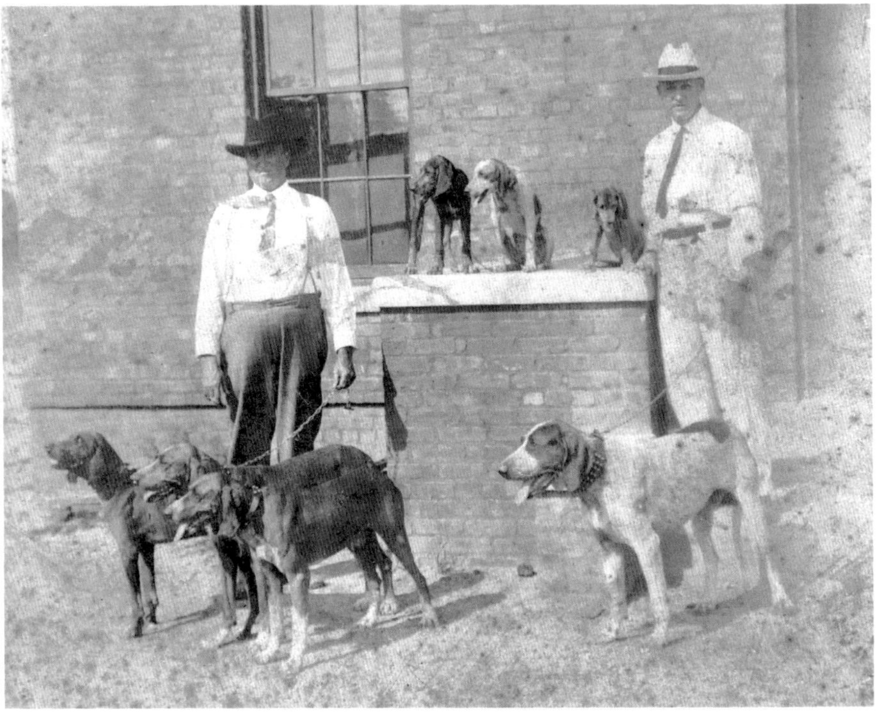

Baldwin County sheriff with his dogs trained to track escapees. *Courtesy of John Lewis.*

has a cemetery cleaning and Decoration Day, someone finds chicken or ham bones somewhere in the cemetery.

Of course, the wind among the grave markers can sound a lot like the eerie sounds of one who lived in the past crying, "Repent." And wild animals could have left bones neatly piled on an unmarked grave.

Located at 64400 Danny Hall Road (County Road 80). From Highway 59 at Tensaw, go east on County Road 80 for 0.2 miles. The cemetery is located behind the Montgomery Hill Baptist Church on the south side of the road. The Montgomery Hill church building has been beautifully restored. The church cornerstone reads, "1854–1972." A wrought-iron arch in front of the church reads, "1840–1972."

Barefoot Annie Hide-and-Seek: The Morris Farm

There is nothing that says "country home" more than the sound of bare feet running across the wooden floor of a porch surrounding the house. That is exactly what makes the Morris Farm in Stockton special to all who believe. And the Morris family certainly believes, for they have stories to share about the little girl whose bare feet are not only heard but also seen!

When we in the South say "porch," we do not mean anything as grand as a veranda. We mean the large room just outside the door. Porches give the house its welcome room, a place to come out of the sun or rain, sit a spell and have a glass of sweet iced tea. More time is spent on the porch than in any of the other rooms of the country house. Peas are shelled there, pecans cracked, games played and memories made. One little girl had such wonderful memories made on that porch and in the farmhouse that she returns often to visit, always bringing a wonderful sense of playful fun and happiness.

Her name is Annie, and she does not like to wear her shoes. Her feet can be heard *pitter-pattering* around the porch gracing two sides of the house. She plays hide-and-seek with her beloved dog, hiding behind the swing hung on the corner of the porch, and runs up and down the porch. She is a five-year-old charmer with cotton-top blond hair, tangled in the back as a little girl's hair is wont to do. It flips up at shoulder level. She wears a dress with aqua and white stripes adorned with puffed sleeves and a collar. Annie lives in the house just as surely as the Morris family does. In fact, she made herself known to Bill even before he bought the place.

In 2005, Scarlet told her father, Bill, that there was an estate sale in Stockton. Interested in the antiques that might be for sale, he and his wife drove from Bay Minette to the Bryant homeplace. As soon as he parked the car on the dirt drive, he told his wife that he was going to buy that house. She thought he was crazy, but he did buy it that very day—the house, three outbuildings and four acres. The occupants of the house at that time were the Ivy family, who were returning to Texas. They had bought it from Harry Bryant, a descendant of the original inhabitants, William and Maggie Bryant, who moved from Mobile. They had ten thousand acres going all the way to the river and had major riverboat docks at both Upper and Lower Bryant's Landing. They bought the land from a man named Vaughn, who had owned the land before the War Between the States. Vaughn is the earliest recorded owner of the property, and he had quite a large plantation worked by many slaves. After the war, when the slaves of his plantation were freed, he deeded them land from the acreage of his plantation. That settlement, named Vaughn, is home to many descendants of those slaves today.

The Vaughns built a small house in 1851, still standing today. The original barn from 1851 is also still standing, as is the smokehouse, which was added in 1890. This plantation was on the Old Federal Road, with a stagecoach transfer station at the Mixon place just south of the Vaughns. The barn was also used as a livery during the war.

The Bryants (William and Maggie) began building the big house facing the road in 1911 and lived their lives there, farming and raising a fine family. The parcel that their children called the homeplace was sixty acres, but they included only six with the house when they sold it to the Ivys. The house is one story but has an enormous attic. In the old days, the yard was enclosed by a picket fence to keep out the free-range cattle. Most homes of that era kept their yards swept clean of grass and rocks. As there were no lawn mowers at that time, a swept yard enabled the family to easily see snakes that might be around. The porch, which is about three feet off the ground, did not have a railing for much of its existence. There were many fruit trees in the yard near the house, and giant ancient fig trees are still alive and are loaded with fruit each year.

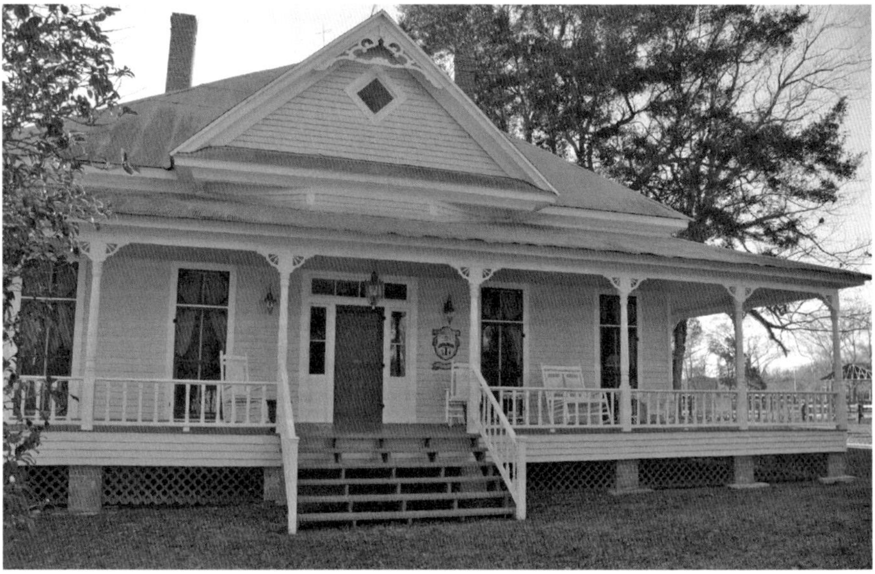

The Morris-Bryant-Vaughn plantation home in Stockton, Alabama. *Photo by Penny H. Taylor.*

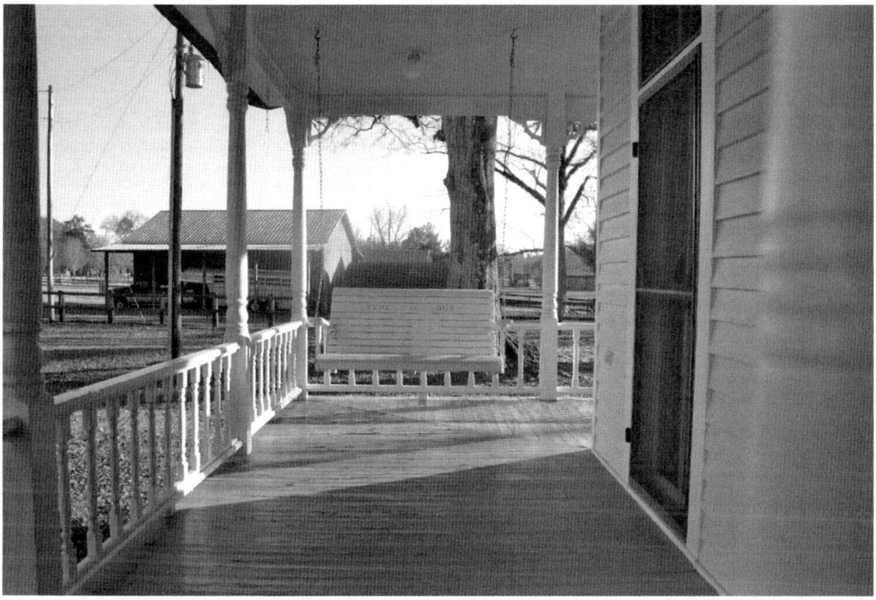

Barefoot Annie's favorite hiding place: the swing on the Morris farmhouse front porch. *Photo by Penny H. Taylor.*

The first encounter with the beautiful little girl happened on the very day Bill bought the house. He was inside the house when his cellphone rang. He walked toward the rear of the house, where there is a side door to the porch, to have his phone conversation with the Federal Emergency Management Agency (FEMA) about a project he was working on. His granddaughters were with him that day, so when he felt a child lean against the back of his leg, he assumed it was one of them. He reached to pat her head, and as he looked at her, he saw a blond child who was not his granddaughter. She then disappeared. He took that as a confirmation that he should go through with the purchase of the house.

After the purchase, work began on the place immediately with the assistance of two faithful, longtime helpers, Virgil and James. They backed a pickup to the front door, where they were going to unload a big oak desk up the stairs and into the house. James had his back to Mr. Morris, and Virgil was looking toward the corner of the porch, where there has always been a porch swing. When Mr. Morris came toward the men, he saw that Virgil was upset, and he asked what was wrong. Virgil had seen a little girl run to the porch swing and then just disappear. He said he had never seen anything like that before.

Immediately after that, Scarlet and Lynn, Bill's daughters who had been cleaning the bathroom on the east side of the house, came out the front door to ask if the men had seen a little girl. They had heard running footsteps on the porch and assumed it was Scarlet's two-year-old son, Hamp, but when they looked, they saw the little girl run from the front porch swing past the window of the bathroom and then disappear. They could not see her feet, but they did see a dog run after her. When they went out to the side porch, they could still see the dog, which ran down the steps into the backyard, but the little girl was gone. The dog stayed around a long time after that, so the dog was "real." Scarlet and Lynn had both seen the same thing.

Soon after that, Hamp was spending the night with his grandparents at the farm, and Mr. Morris heard Hamp playing in the front parlor, happily talking with a playmate. When Mr. Morris went in there, there was no one else there, and he asked Hamp who he was talking to. Hamp said, "I was playing with Annie." Grandpa asked, "Where is she now?" Then Hamp took Mr. Morris across the hall into another bedroom and showed him the door that Annie had gone through, a closet access to the attic by means of a crude ladder. That was ten years ago, and Hamp still remembers her clearly.

One day soon after that, Scarlet was in the kitchen making a picnic to take to her children, who were playing in the creek in the back. She heard a little voice call, "Mama," through the screen door. She said, "Come on in, Sarah." When she went to the door to check on Sarah, there was no one there. Another morning, while Scarlet and her family were spending the night there, her husband, Hamilton, was awakened very early in the morning by one of the girls calling, "Mama…Mama." He walked into the front bedroom, where their two girls were sound asleep, not even restless. This is the same room in which Hamp had seen Annie walk to the door leading to the attic. Neither girl had ever talked in her sleep before, so Hamilton felt sure that Annie had been in there calling her mother.

One Mother's Day, Mr. Morris came into the house through the kitchen door and went to disarm the security system. Then something caught his eye up on the ceiling. There was a magnificent footprint of a barefoot child. The footprint was dark, like the child had played in the dirt or soot. The toes were perfect. It was there until Mr. Morris had the ceiling painted—the workers did not realize that the footprint was a treasure and painted over it. Mr. Morris and his two workers have often noticed Annie playing in the yard or running on the porch, and when they make eye contact with her, she disappears. Usually footsteps are heard before she makes an appearance. So the feet are very important in understanding why Annie visits the Morris

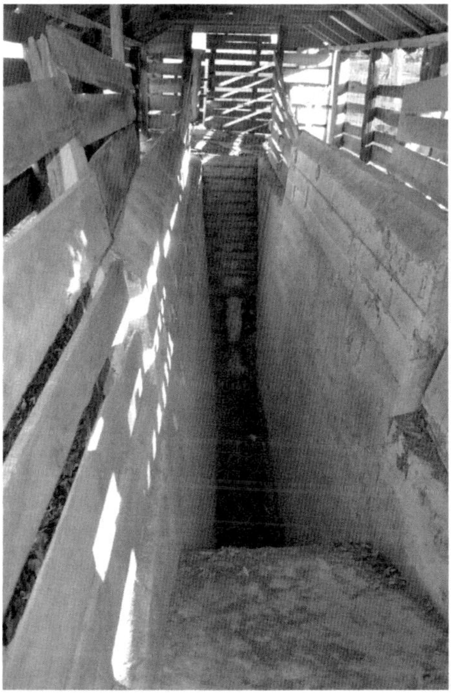

Dipping vat used to treat cows for disease-carrying pests. *Photo by Penny H. Taylor.*

home. Also, calling for "Mama" is indicative that she needs to ask her mother something.

Who is Annie? The dipping vat may hold a clue to the date and her age. Dipping vats were built throughout the South to treat cattle for Texas fever carried by ticks. DDT was put in water in a narrow cement trough, and cattle were forced down the slanted end into the water, where they instinctively swam to the other end. A vat had been built here on the farm so the cattle could be treated without driving them a long distance to the nearest government vat. There in the cement of the floor of the slab are two perfect prints of a five-year-old girl. The date is legible there: 1910.

Neighbors around have said it was rumored that a child visiting there fell off the porch, broke her neck and consequently died. Perhaps that child loved the farmhouse dearly and comes there for visits often. Mrs. Bryant was a Richerson, a prominent family in the community, with a family cemetery in Stockton. There was a tragic death of a two-year-old girl who is buried there, but Annie appears to be closer to five or six years old.

They haven't seen Annie lately. Perhaps the children are too old to be her playmates, and she will wait until there are grandchildren once again running in the house before she comes back for a play date. The Morris family emphasizes that there is a wonderful, happy feeling in the house. There are no sinister vibrations, and Annie brings wonder and laughter with her visits. They feel that she is pleased that Mr. Morris worked to re-create the place as it was in 1911, so she comes to play.

The Morris family farm now encompasses the sixty acres that were considered part of the homeplace and has fenced the entire property; a herd of cattle grazes there. It is once again truly a working farm. The house feels just like it did when it was new. Beautiful period furniture

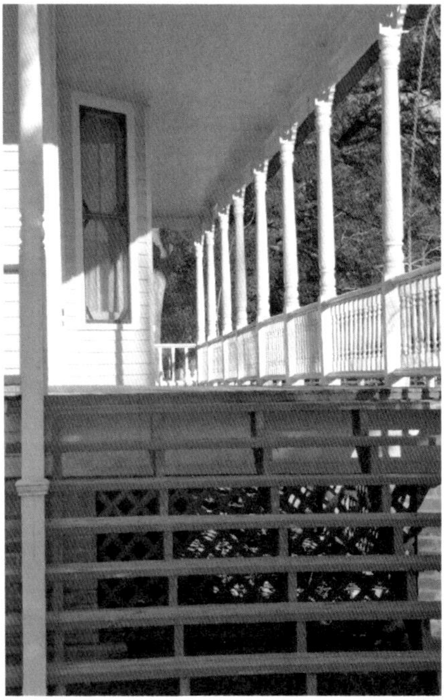

The front porch steps, Morris Farm, Stockton, Alabama. *Photo by Penny H. Taylor.*

graces the large rooms, which have been completely restored to their original elegance. Mr. Morris found a piece of a picket fence in the barn and had it replicated to enclose the yard, and he has replaced the porch rail that was once there, thus ensuring that no child falls off. The porch swing has been there for one hundred years, and the steps are exactly the same. Walking up the steps to the front porch takes everyone who comes there back a century to visit with friends and family and maybe see Annie play hide-and-seek. Take off your shoes and sit a spell.

The Morris family home is a private residence located on Bryant Landing Road in Stockton and is marked with information on a historic marker.

MASSACRE AT FORT MIMS: TENSAW

The grounds at the site of the greatest massacre in United States history still carry a sense of forbidding menace. The echoes of screams of settlers and war whoops of Creek Indians reverberate throughout the wilderness there in the northernmost part of Baldwin County. More people claim to have had eerie experiences here than in any other place in Baldwin County, except perhaps at Fort Morgan. Death and destruction have left timeless messages of impending death at this place.

The massacre marked the beginning of the Creek Indian Wars, a facet of the War of 1812. The Creek nation was incited by the British to attack American settlers encroaching on their lands. Even after a visit by Chief Tecumseh, the Creek nation was divided. It is important to note that many people in this area were of mixed blood, and the Americans and Indians were often related. A vote was held among the Creeks for or against war, using white or red sticks. Those wanting to fight the Americans won the vote and were therefore called "Red Sticks." Among their leaders was the famous Red Eagle, or William Weatherford, who was not a chief but was greatly respected.

After a group of Creek Indians was attacked by Americans at Burnt Corn Creek, the Indians were further incited to attack. As news of the unrest among the Creeks spread, Americans in Tensaw were alarmed, and many moved their families to the homestead of neighbor Samuel Mims on the banks of Boatyard Lake, an old channel of the Alabama River. A contingency of 265 soldiers was sent to Fort Mims to help protect the settlers there, and a stockade was built around about an acre of the Mims farm, including the Mims house. Living in the seventeen buildings and many military tents were about 265 soldiers and at least 553 settlers.

Commanding the fort was Major Daniel Beasley, whose actions showed that he was not up to the job of protecting the fort. Beasley had become complacent—some historians even call him arrogant—regarding the threat of an Indian attack. He blatantly ignored reports of the threat. Failure to heed the warnings resulted in lack of preparation for the Indian attack on August 30, 1813, which historians call one of the bloodiest horrors to take place on American soil. It is generally agreed that between 250 and 400 settlers and militiamen were scalped and murdered. Although scalping was not a common Creek practice, the rumor that the British were offering to pay five dollars per scalp motivated the gruesome mutilations. The Creek Indians captured 100 to 150 slaves who were living in the compound. The Creeks also suffered major losses, perhaps up to 300, bravely fighting for their homelands.

Today, the fort is designated as a historic site, and the Fort Mims Restoration Association has rebuilt a blockhouse and a part of the stockade and placed four large markers. The group sponsors a reenactment of the battle in August of each year; the smell of smoke is not only from the black powder of the reenactors' muskets but also residual odor of burning buildings and bodies. As one walks there, feet tread on ground that once soaked up the blood of victims who have stories to tell and unfinished business. Paranormal investigators have spent numerous evenings here recording and communicating with some of those victims and perhaps even the attackers. Voices are clearly heard, apparitions are seen and many, many orbs move about the battlefield.

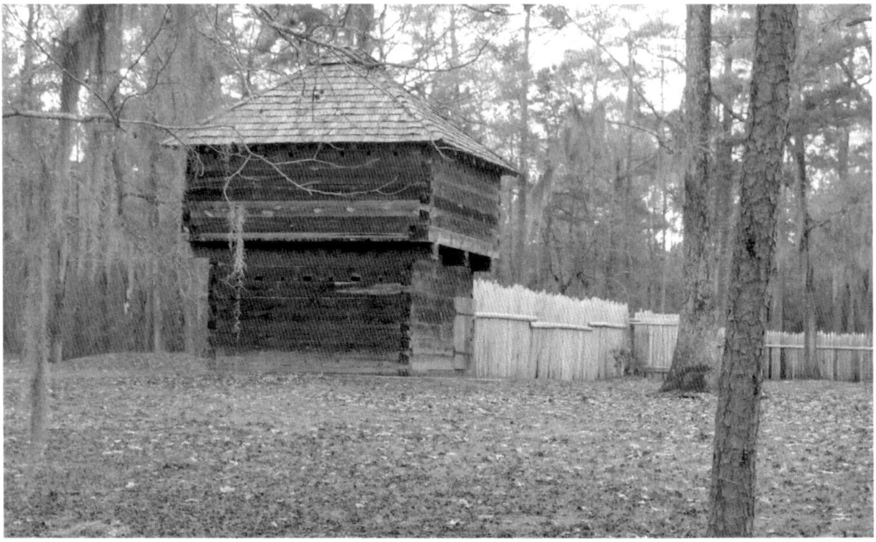

Reproduction blockhouse constructed at the Fort Mims Massacre Historic Site by the Fort Mims Preservation Association. *Photo by Penny H. Taylor.*

One of the members of the restoration association reported the following:

> *A couple of years ago, we allowed a group of paranormal investigators to stay overnight. My granddaughter and I visited them just as a storm was rolling in. We were huddled arm in arm a little cold and a little uneasy. They were wide-eyed when they told us they saw a figure of a man at the East Gate…thought it was someone playing a joke on them, but there was no one around. They also tried recording and called out Major Beasley's name and got plenty of reply. The recordings were eerie but occasionally words that I could understand…I decided not to stick around. Being in the mist and seeing orbs all around was really strange.*

The hauntings witnessed seem to be warnings of the impending attack. In fact, in 1813, warnings were repeatedly relayed and consistently ignored. Perhaps these frustrated returning spirits are once again warning of danger, hoping that this time the alarms will not fall on deaf ears. One such warning was issued by General Claiborne, who was in charge of the defense of the region. After he visited Fort Mims on August 7, he wrote to Beasley instructing him to increase the fortifications and build at least three more blockhouses, stating that "to respect our Enemy and to prepare in the best possible way to meet him, is the certain means to ensure success." Beasley, however, did not feel any impending danger and did nothing to strengthen the fort other than construct a second defensive wall facing the East Gate.

Another warning came the day before the massacre when two slaves reported that they had seen braves in war paint in the woods while they were outside the fort tending cattle. To his credit, Beasley did send a scouting party of ten outside the enclosure. Two of these scouts rode within three hundred yards of the camouflaged Creeks, who could hear the men talking. When the scouts brought back reports of no danger, Beasley ordered the slaves whipped. The owner of one of the slaves believed his trusted friend and would not allow the beating to take place, but the other received painful lashes with a leather whip. Some of the sounds recorded by investigators seem to be a voice pleading in distress. Those listening feel that they are being warned to flee.

The appearances of orbs are common at the site, many at eye level along the walls of the fort. In constructing the pine log stockade, a deadly mistake was made. The gun slits were cut at eye level rather than on a raised platform. This gave the Indians a way to peer into the fort the night before and observe the soldiers and settlers drinking whiskey and rowdily playing cards. The Indians then planned to man the slits from the outside before they could be manned from the inside by the soldiers.

An apparition at the gate is one of the most powerful indicators of the return of spirits to the battlefield. This may be a messenger who was not there for the battle but whose one last warning was scoffed by the militia. Before noon, James Cornell, a scout,

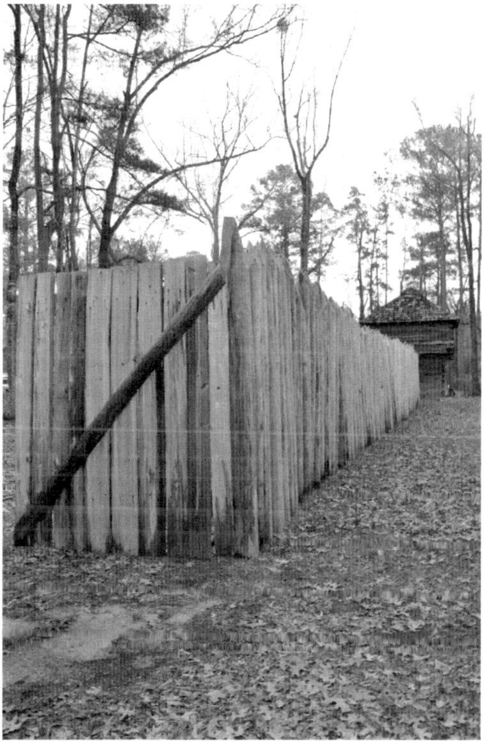

The Fort Mims stockade gate was wedged open by sand, preventing its closure. *Photo by Penny H. Taylor.*

galloped into the fort shouting to Major Beasley that the war party was advancing toward Fort Mims. Beasley, who was probably drunk, mocked Cornell, saying that he must have seen red cattle. Cornell yelled back at the major that those red cattle would "give you one hell of a kick before nightfall." Major Beasley ordered Cornell arrested, but he turned and fled, escaping the soldiers and leaving the fort to its fate. He had made the statement that if the men were to prepare to fight, he would stay and join them to his death, but if the contingency were to remain unprepared, he would take no part in the battle.

The Indians were waiting in a ravine ready to attack at the lunch hour on August 30, 1813. When the drums sounded dinner, it was the death knoll. The Red Sticks made their approach. If there were any Indian voices raised in bloodcurdling war screams, they were drowned out by the music and drums inside the fort. The Creeks rushed to the gun slits and into the fort through the East Gate, which was wedged open by shifting sand. Some think that perhaps the Creeks had even put the dirt against the gate during the previous night. Beasley did exhibit honor at this last moment, drawing his sword and attempting to close the gate. He was killed immediately. Despite the number of attackers, the settlers were able to hold the fort behind the secondary wall of defense for quite a while. Cabins were set afire by flaming arrows, and the screams of settlers were accompanied by the sounds of hand-to-hand combat until about 3:00 p.m. The exhausted Indians left the fort to regroup in the woods. The surviving settlers gathered in the loomhouse on the northern side of the wall. The Indian leaders rallied the Red Sticks to resume their attack with renewed frenzy, setting the loomhouse afire and bringing an end to the battle. The sun set on the gory scene; very few settlers had escaped the massacre.

There are several reports of Indians showing mercy and concern for the settlers. Red Eagle, appalled at the brutality toward the women and children, tried to calm the warriors and actually left the fort to meet his brother, David Tate, twenty miles north of the fort that afternoon. Jahomobtee reportedly shot three warriors who were attacking women and children. One woman was recognized by Dog Warrior, whom she had befriended in his childhood. He led her and two children to safety outside the fort. Several settlers escaped, some through a hole in the stockade near the loomhouse, where the settlers were holed up during the final phases of the battle.

News of the attack spread rapidly, with some reports made by those at nearby Fort Pierce who could hear the gunfire and explosions and some by those who had escaped and made their way across the river to Fort

Stoddert. On September 9, a contingency of men under the command of Major Kennedy arrived at the gruesome scene to bury the dead. The description of the compound is beyond comprehension. They found what was left of hundreds of human bodies. They had been burned, mutilated and left to the elements of nature for several days. The soldiers dug a trench, put the decimated remains in it and covered them with a thin layer of dirt. They also found evidence that hundreds of warriors were buried in a trench outside the walls.

Historians have researched, interviewed and studied primary accounts of the battle. Their extensive body of work reflects the magnitude of the Fort Mims Massacre from the historical standpoint. However, those who seek the deeper truths go to the fort on a night when the sky is a black velvet sheet dotted with pinholes of pain that are wont to cry out. Those in wait have a tingling in their fingertips and chills on their necks as they sense the impending death scene. Fort Mims is one of those places where only the brave or the foolish fail to heed the warnings of coming doom. Beware! Leave now while you can.

For more information on Fort Mims sightings, see Haunted Alabama Battlefields *by Dale Langella, published by The History Press, 2013. The Fort Mims website can be found at www.fortmims.org.*

Little Red Schoolhouse: Bay Minette

A beautiful little girl was born in 1881 to a black family near Selma, Alabama. Her parents were determined to give her a life they could never have. They had been slaves as children on a plantation here but now were sharecroppers—still a hard life, but they were free and could make plans for dreams to come true. They raised their Rebecca with a strong emphasis on education, making sacrifices to send her to school so that she could learn to read and write. She was one of those rare girls who finished high school and earned her teaching certificate due to her parents' hard work and her own self-determination.

When she met George, she fell in love and they planned a future together. They moved to Baldwin County, where George worked in the Sibley Mill at Bromley, and soon saved enough to buy land and build a home there.

As the couple was blessed with children, Rebecca began to teach them at home, as there was no school building in which they could have lessons. As the community grew, friends and family asked Rebecca to teach their children, and the class soon outgrew the kitchen of their home. After World War I, the men of the community responded to Rebecca's pleas for a school. They went to see the school superintendent, Samuel Tharp, in 1919 to ask for a school and were told that if the community built the school, the county would pay the teacher.

Magnolia Baptist Church in Bromley was connected with the Eastern Shore Baptist Missionary Association in Daphne, which had built the first school for black children in Baldwin County. The association assisted the Bromley community in securing a grant from the Julius Rosenwald Fund. The president of Sears, Roebuck and Company had set up funds to build schools for children of former slaves. The Magnolia Baptist Church applied for the funds through Tuskegee Institute, which was managing the program at that time. It was awarded $400, to be matched through local supplies and services of the community.

So those men and women went to work, cutting trees from their property and using their peckerwood sawmill to plane the boards; they erected a one-room schoolhouse to rival all others in the county. It was built using the plans borrowed from the school across the road built for white children. The new school was painted with a red paint developed by Mr. George Washington Carver at Tuskegee, so it was dubbed the Little Red Schoolhouse and was known in the community as the "Bromley School." School system records, however, designated the school as the Blakeley School, as the Bromley School listed on official inventories was for white children.

Ms. Rebecca taught those children with all her heart. She taught grades one through eight—her own children, her nieces and nephews, her grandchildren and all the neighbors' children. George converted his pickup truck into a makeshift bus and crossed Bromley Creek at the ford on Bromley Road to help transport those children who lived too far away to walk to school. Memories of those students focus on the loving discipline of Ms. Rebecca. There were actually two regular teachers there at the school for several years, and others were in and out for short periods of time.

Many of the students who finished the eight grades in Bromley School went on to attend high school at Baldwin County Training School in Daphne, the only high school for black children at that time. Graduates of that school have become some of the most outstanding leaders and educators in Baldwin County. The Little Red Schoolhouse stayed open until 1950, when

Douglasville School (Bay Minette) was expanded to include a high school, whereupon the schoolhouse was consolidated and closed. The children were transported to Douglasville, but Mr. George was still their bus driver, and Ms. Rebecca was a teacher there, so home folks were still present to continue the legacy of excellence in education. Ms. Rebecca taught in the school system for more than fifty years, and there are at least fifty descendants of this couple who are in the Baldwin County school system.

The lonely Little Red Schoolhouse stood abandoned on Magnolia Church Road until it was sorely needed at White House Fork to house a kindergarten class in 1980. The school was moved and insulated, and a tile floor was installed. The front stoop and cupola were added, with the redwood school bell made by the vocational school students hanging proudly on the porch. Many children there were lovingly taught their basics by Mrs. Ryan, who worked there for at least ten years.

When a new school at White House Fork, Delta Elementary, was built in 1990, the little school was saved by one of Rebecca's grandsons, Sam Watson, and a former superintendent, Leslie Smith. The building was moved to the school system office complex in Bay Minette and was

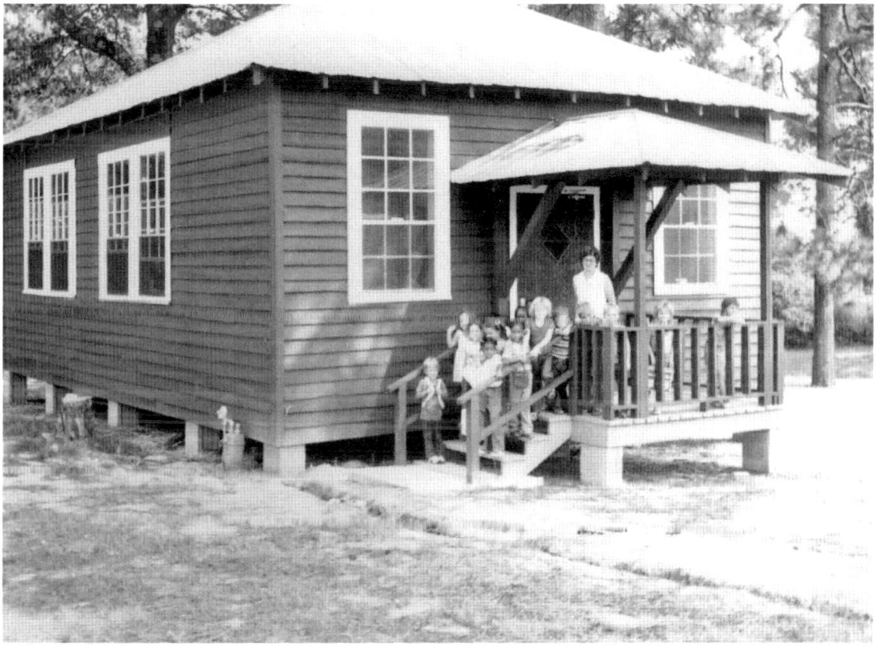

Bromley School on Magnolia Church Road was moved to White House Fork school in 1980 and was used as a kindergarten classroom, as pictured here. *Author's collection.*

lovingly restored and furnished with the help of a foundation organized to preserve it. It was saved but not used very much until 2005, when the school superintendent asked to have it refurbished and opened to students for field trips. A renewed interest resulted in a living history museum where classes came to experience a typical school day as it had been in 1921. The living history program became an immediate success, with student field trips held there every week during the school year, with students and teachers dressed in early 1920s garb.

Volunteers served as schoolmarms who conducted class just as it would have been done in 1921, when the school opened. Children had to file in line and stand at their desks until the teacher gave them permission to be seated. Children were assigned roles to play in the day's activities. Some had to fill the water bucket from the hand pump. Some fed the furnace and swept the floor. Others had to clean the blackboards. All children did their lessons on slate boards and stood for oral reading and for the old-fashioned spelling bee. The recitation bench at the front of the room was used for the children to recite their memory verses to the teacher. Sometimes it seemed almost as if the class really had traveled back in time.

Many days when the volunteer schoolmarm arrived to prepare for class for the day, she found that there was a wonderful feeling in the building. The

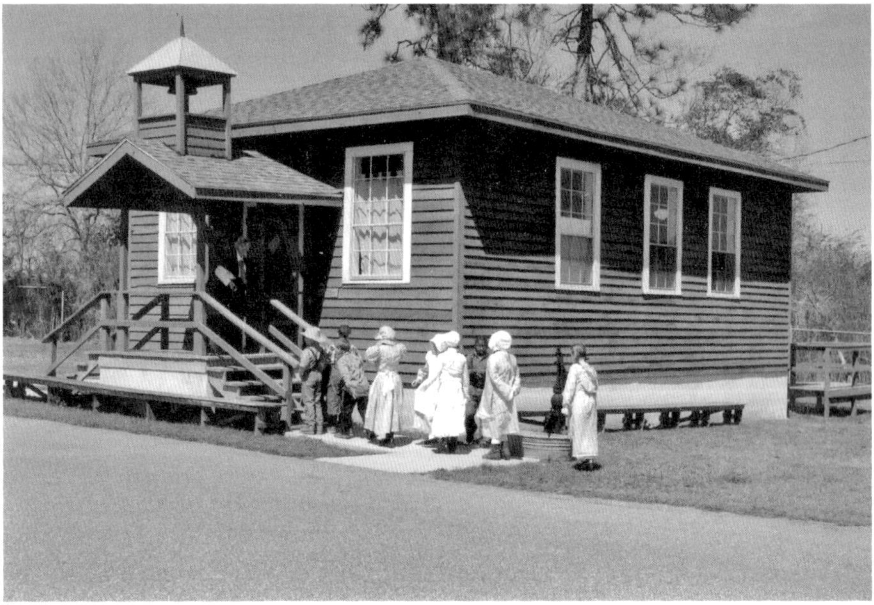

Bromley School after it was moved to the Baldwin County Public Schools Office Complex in Bay Minette. *Photo by Fran Campbell.*

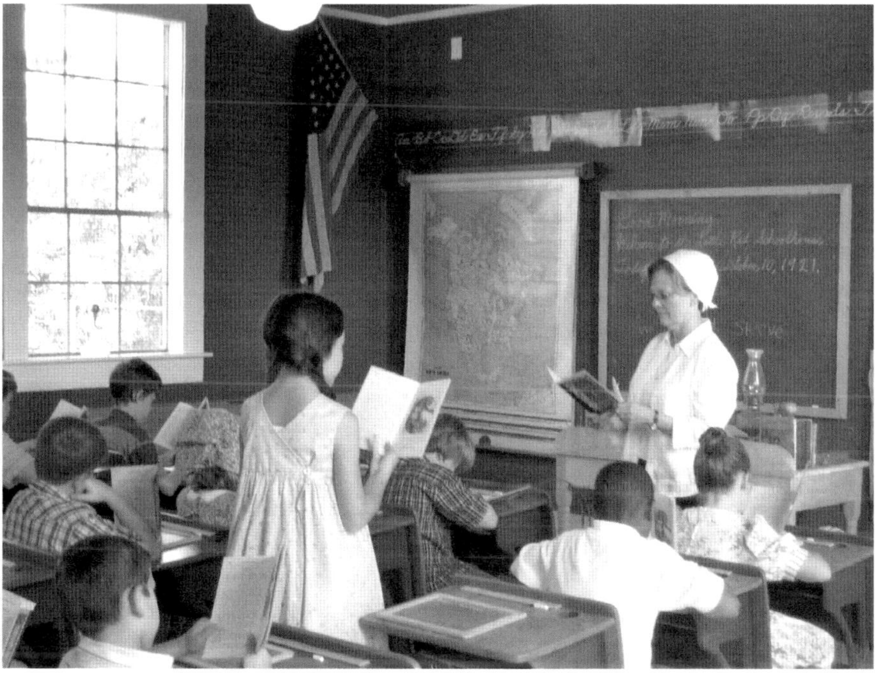

Reenactment school day classes held in the one-room Little Red Schoolhouse, Bay Minette. *Photo by Fran Campbell.*

temperature was almost always perfect in this little treasure. One morning, when she arrived, there were arithmetic problems written on the slate board in perfect penmanship. She assumed that others had been in the building, so she erased them and went on with the day as planned. The following week, when she arrived, she noticed that the "ABC" blocks on the side table were arranged in order a perfect line of the alphabet. She thought that the children of a custodian or other officeworker must have been playing there sometime during the week. On another day, the portrait of George Washington had been raised out of the reach of little hands, and the teacher's desk had been straightened and cleaned.

One day, the Holy Bible was opened to Psalms on the teacher's desk. The schoolmarm began to feel a presence there and looked forward to the next visit to see what the unseen teacher was saying to her. Soon after, the schoolmarm found a book on the recitation bench. She knew that the book had been in the library cabinet at the rear of the schoolhouse the prior week. The book was opened to the cover sheet, and she read the inscription written in the book: "Bromley School #14/Seven Day Book." This book had actually been used by those teachers in Bromley and had remained there during the school's tenure at White House Fork, and no one had ever realized that this book was one of the originals. The volunteer took the book with her to the archives for cataloguing and preservation of this rare artifact. The very next week, the most amazing incident occurred. The volunteer schoolmarm came into the room to find words written with a finger in the dust on the slate board: "Where is…." Needless to say, the book was returned to the Little Red Schoolhouse and left there for the unseen teacher, whoever she is, to use as she teaches her many pupils who must come there for their lessons. The saying that teachers never die is certainly true in this special place.

Those teachers who taught here in the past are present today as surely as they were here in days gone by. A sense of place is now joined by a sense of legacy that will live forever. This is one of those spots where the past and the present meet.

The Little Red Schoolhouse is located on Hand Avenue in Bay Minette on the Baldwin County Public Schools Central Office Campus. It is open by appointment through the Superintendent's Office. See the website at www.bcbe.org. The site is designated with a historic marker, reading as follows:

> *PUBLIC EDUCATION IN BALDWIN COUNTY*
>
> *In 1799 the first public school in Alabama was built just north of this site at Boatyard Lake in the Tensaw Community. More than 90 small schools dotted Baldwin County in the early twentieth century. This one room school was built in 1920 by African American families in Bromley, and served grades 1–9. It was moved to White House Fork in 1970, and used as a kindergarten room until 1990. It has been preserved here under the leadership of Sam Watson and Leslie Smith as a tribute to community education in Baldwin County. It is dedicated to Mrs. Rebecca Tompkins, principal and teacher of the Blakeley Little Red Schoolhouse.*
>
> *Dedicated August 2008*

A Ghost Town: Blakeley

There is a real ghost town in Baldwin County. Come with me as we walk down dirt roads that were once lined with thriving businesses, hotels, a newspaper office, a courthouse and many beautiful homes. None of those structures remains here, but if you pay close attention, you can sense their presence, as well as those of some of the most colorful people of Alabama. Blakeley was one of the earliest "planned communities" in the South, the brainchild of Josiah Blakeley. On the banks of the Tensaw River on the eastern side of the Mobile Bay Delta, Josiah purchased a huge tract of land—here he would fulfill his lifelong dream of building a city. He hired a surveyor and finalized the plat for the new town in 1813. Plans were implemented to build homes and businesses, and the town of Blakeley was soon to rival the port of Mobile. Josiah was totally immersed in the development of the town. He built a small house there and hired crews to clear the land, laying out the roads around two public squares. Within a year, the town had a sizeable population and took on its character.

Josiah was at last satisfied that his work would be a legacy for the future of America. This town bearing his name gave him a great sense of accomplishment. As with so many great men who do not live to see the fruits of their labors, Josiah was killed just one year later. One day, while riding through the construction sites, he decided to survey the outlying perimeter of the town. His horse evidently was frightened or stepped in a gopher hole, and Josiah was thrown from his horse and broke his neck. At least, that is what those who found his body assumed. No one is sure where his body was buried, but it would have made sense to think it was in the town cemetery, near where his body was found.

Former park ranger David is pretty sure he knows. In fact, David has always wanted to pay tribute to the man who founded the town but did not live to see its success. David knows all about Josiah and is sure that he has a special bond with him. He is one of the few people who actively seeks information about Josiah's elusive death and burial. David is most communicative about his encounters with the spirits haunting Blakeley, but one stands out in his mind because he caught it on his phone camera. One day, as he was in the guard shed near the cemetery, he felt an urge to go outside. A magnetic force pulled him from his desk and took him onto the porch, and his feet took him to the east end of the shed. There, in a seemingly unpretentious location, a column of steam began to rise from the ground. The steam or vapor formed a whirlwind over that spot on the ground. David approached the column and was standing in the midst of the fog, where he heard the moaning of the long-lost founder of Blakeley. There was no doubt in his mind that this is either the place where Josiah was thrown from his horse or his final resting place.

Judge and Jury

Let us continue our walk down the dirt roads toward the center of town. As the road turns to the right, we see a marker signifying the former location of the large oak tree that was the center of justice for the area while still under the Mississippi Territory rule. This tree stood until it was damaged by Hurricane Frederic in 1979 and later fell in 1992. By 1811, this was the site of the Superior Court, with Judge Harry Toulmin presiding. Legend has it that Judge Toulmin sat on a low limb of the oak tree to hear the cases, and from this bench his sentences were issued. John M. tells time and time again that as he stood on the spot where the mighty Jury Oak once stood, he distinctly heard the word *guilty* over and over.

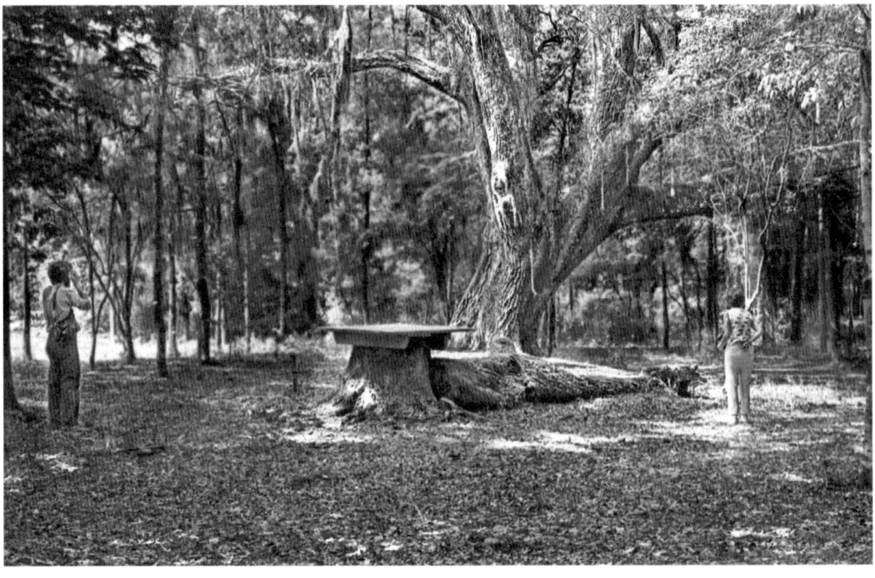

Jury Oak, Blakeley. Judge Toulmin sat on the branches and held court before the courthouse was built. *Author's collection.*

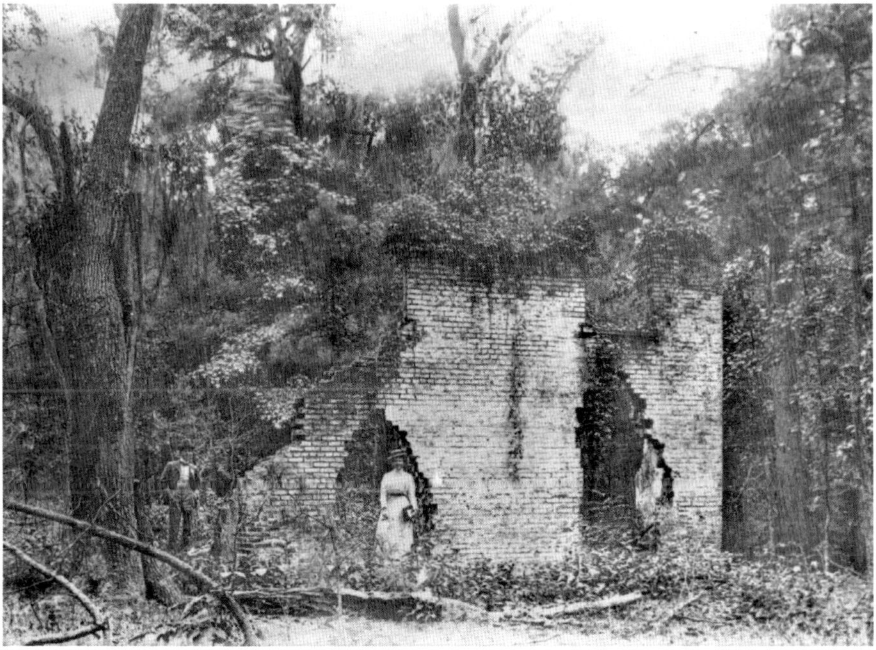

Blakeley Courthouse ruins, circa 1890. *Courtesy of University of South Alabama Archives.*

A fine brick courthouse was built in 1820; soon after, Blakeley was officially named the county seat, having already been the seat of the federal Superior Court sessions for at least ten years. Blakeley remained the county seat long after the town had been all but abandoned and was still in use during the famous Battle of Blakeley. Soon after the war, the county seat was officially moved to the Eastern Shore town of Daphne. The Blakeley Courthouse fell into ruins, and the site became known for its hauntings. Thrill-seekers of the Gay Nineties came by boat from Mobile to try their luck at seeing apparitions or hearing sounds from the past. Brave young men often camped there at the courthouse site overnight. One story surfaced in which the narrator, Alan B., described the night's experience as frightening. He reported that he and his friends did not see anything early in the evening, but when it was nearly dawn, they were awakened by the sound of iron doors crashing shut and the ground shaking beneath them. The jail, which was below ground level, had already filled in, but evidently the sounds were coming from beneath where the men were sleeping. The vibrations woke all of the campers, each of whom felt the sensation of a mild earthquake. One said that a few of the bricks toppled from the ruins of one of the walls.

As nature continued to reclaim the once thriving town, the courthouse site became undetectable to the naked eye. It continued to be rumored that sightseers to the ghost town might experience the ground shaking. Artifact hunters and relic seekers plundered the town and battlefield for years before it became protected thanks to the foresight of a group of people who formed a foundation to save it. As visitors walk the dirt streets, the location of the onetime bustling courthouse is clearly marked. The park closes at dark, but a group of ghost hunters got permission to stay overnight to glean readings if possible. One of those in the party ended up sleeping alone in her car. She said she was awakened by a shaking sensation. She believes.

The Hanging Tree

Of all the many haunts at Blakeley, the Hanging Tree remains one of the most famous. Many people have said that the orbs there are frightening and that they have even photographed them. If a death sentence was administered to a prisoner, he would have been sentenced to be hanged from a huge oak tree that still stands today. Rather than construct gallows in the town, the judge decided to make use of the mighty branches of one of the live oaks abundant in the area. A live oak has branches that curve and take on mystical shapes. Usually Spanish moss thrives on the limbs and lends an even more ominous aura to the tree at night. A few of the original trees still stand in the Blakeley State Park, but most were cleared out during the preparation for the Battle of Blakeley at the end of the great War Between the States. The Hanging Tree was spared. It is probably nearly 250 years old now.

The number of hangings that took place there at Blakeley is not known, but from the numbers of orbs often witnessed there, it must be concluded that hundreds occurred. In the early days here, justice was swift and not always sure. Stories of men unjustly hanged were told. Perhaps those are some of the brightest orbs making themselves seen on dark nights at Blakeley.

The Battle of Blakeley

The city of Blakeley was not to survive. It was all but abandoned due to several yellow fever epidemics and loss of shipping business. Many buildings were dismantled and moved to Mobile, giving it the appearance of a ghost town by the time of the Civil War. By far the most well-known facet of the town's history is the Battle of Blakeley, one of the final battles of the war, fought here on April 9. It began in the evening of the very day that General Lee surrendered at Appomattox Court House. The extensive earthworks still in existence are reminders of the bloody encounter that took place. So many people have witnessed the apparition of a young boy wearing a Confederate hat that he has been given a name: Jeremy.

Jeremy was taken under the wings of the soldiers there at Redoubt No. 4. He was a local ten-year-old boy who was fascinated by the life of the soldiers and took to hanging around their campsite. One of the soldiers even gave him an old Confederate kepi that he had saved from a slain comrade. Jeremy happened to be leaving the campsite to return to his nearby cabin when the Union army set siege. Jeremy wore the cap with such bearing and pride that the Union forces thought he was really an enlisted man and captured him. They forced him to walk into the land in front of the earthworks and pace up and down the field to test it for land mines. He did trip one of those mines and was killed there between the forces. The men in Redoubt No. 4 were devastated at witnessing the cruelty of the Union soldiers, and they were driven to fight even harder in order to honor the young boy. Jeremy is often seen today. He is seen by hikers, by park rangers and by reenactors at the battlefield. In *Haunted Alabama Battlefields*, Dale Langella reported that a park ranger saw him while cutting grass and left the park, never to return. Langella told of the many other apparitions on the battlefield, both Confederate and Yankee. Park Ranger Dave said that campers sometimes see a Confederate soldier relaxing on one of the picnic tables in the campground. In fact, he has witnessed it himself.

Come walk the dirt roads that lead to the past. You may spend the night here and experience the past for yourself.

Blakely State Park is located on Highway 225 north of Spanish Fort. For more information about ghosts at Blakeley, see Haunted Alabama Battlefields *by Dale Langella. The Blakeley State Park website can be found at www.blakeleypark.com.*

PART II
The Eastern Shore of Mobile Bay

When Spaniard Alonso de Pineda sailed into what is now Mobile Bay, he named it Espiritu Santo, or Bay of the Holy Ghost. He cruised the bay for forty days and noted more than forty Indian settlements along the banks. The French were the first to establish a successful European colony here, which was at the Village on the northeastern shores of the bay. Settlements, potteries, brickworks, hotels and plantations grew up all along the shoreline. Many Mobilians built homes here for seasonal escape from the heat and diseases of summer in the city. Each community has its tales, legends and hauntings. Let's tell some.

The Slave Gallery: Daphne Methodist Church Museum

In front of the Daphne City Hall on the Eastern Shore of Mobile Bay, there stands a bronze statue of the Greek goddess Daphne. The myth connects the goddess to the Laurel Tree. In Greek mythology, Apollo insulted the god of love, Eros. In retribution, Eros used two arrows, one of gold to incite love and one of lead to incite hatred. He used the golden arrow to create in Apollo a love for the nymph Daphne, but the leaden one was buried in Daphne's heart, leading her to abhor Apollo. Apollo was not one to quietly accept rejection. He chased the lovely girl throughout the forests she loved.

Daphne's father was the god of the river, Peneus, and he wanted Daphne to marry and bear him grandchildren. Daphne, however, ignored his pleas and continued her life of woodland sports.

At this time, Eros, wanting the entertainment of a good chase, intervened. He empowered Apollo with extra speed, and soon he was gaining on Daphne. As Daphne saw Apollo, she called out to her father, "Please help me, Father. Help me to be free of this moment forever. Open the earth to swallow me." Peneus followed his fatherly inclinations and immediately transformed Daphne into a tree. Her skin became the bark, her arms became branches, her legs became the trunk and her hair was turned into leaves. She was rooted to the ground as Apollo reached her. He reached out to the branches, but they, too, pulled away from him. He still felt an undying love for this beauty and pledged to honor her forever. He used his powers to make her leaves become evergreen and swore to protect her. From then on, he declared that her leaves would be used to make wreaths to adorn the heads of victors and to crown emperors. Thus the myth goes that led to the name of the town on the Eastern Shore of Mobile Bay and to one of its more colorful characters.

Captain and Mrs. William Howard built a large wharf and a magnificent hotel named the Village of Bell Rose, which became well known for its setting and service. As were most ladies of that era, Mrs. Howard was well versed in the classics. When she noticed all of the native laurel trees in the area, she could well imagine the goddess Daphne running through these thick forests. She used the laurel leaves to decorate the hotel and told people the myth. She told them to always be on the lookout for a lovely young woman running in the nearby woods. Just as she expected, one day her eyes fell on a lovely woman drawing fresh water from the nearby spring. She was wearing a wreath of laurel branches that she had fashioned as she walked to the spring. Mrs. Howard approached the woman and discovered that she was a former slave living with the Yancey family on Yancey Branch. As a child, she was saved from the Massacre of Fort Mims by Mrs. Yancey, who had recently died. As the young girl did not know her name or her owner, she was named Nan by Mrs. Yancey, who saw to it that she was given her freedom papers. Mrs. Howard told her the story of the goddess and said that she would always call her Daphne in honor of the myth and her resemblance to a Greek goddess.

Mrs. Howard offered Daphne a position at the Howard Hotel, and Daphne worked diligently, becoming indispensible to its operation. She managed the maintenance and services to the guests, who dearly loved her.

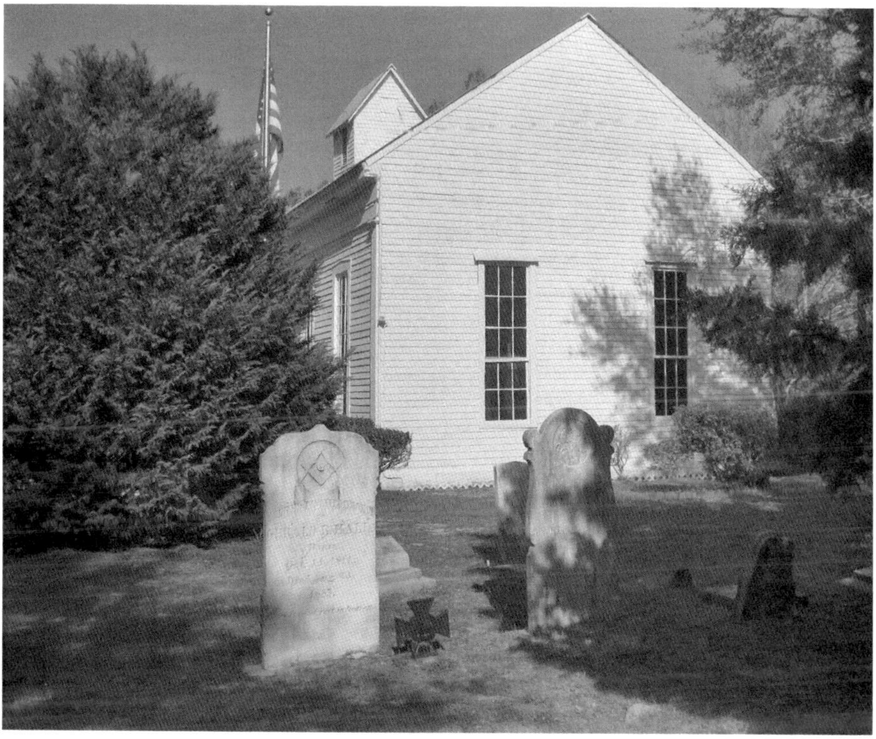

Daphne Methodist Church Museum and Cemetery, Daphne, Alabama. *Photo by the author.*

She helped Mrs. Howard and her friend Josephine Hardwick plant rows of cedar trees all the way from the hotel to the Methodist church.

During her lifetime, many cities in the South were plagued by yellow fever, carried by mosquitoes and prevalent in the marshy lands. The community of Bell Rose did not escape the ravages of a terrible epidemic. Daphne seemed to have an innate sense of nursing and worked around the clock tending patients and restoring most of them to good health. Like the nymph Daphne, she knew the healing properties of plants and the value of fresh water and cleanliness. She is credited with saving the town from the same fate as Blakeley, which fell into ruin after several bouts with the terrifying disease.

Daphne was still alive when the Howards gave the land adjacent to the hotel for a new church to house the Methodist congregation. It was started in the 1850s and completed in 1859. The wonderful building stands today, with its gallery for the African American population who attended. Many of these were slaves, thus the term "slave gallery" is used to define the space upstairs. The upstairs parishioners joined the others in prayer and the singing of hymns. Daphne especially loved the hymn singing and always added her special harmony and rhythm, bringing a sense of her African heritage. Her voice rang out above most in the congregation, and she inspired all who heard her. At times, even during the sermon, Daphne would start humming a lovely melody, which added reverence to the worship service.

The idyllic little town and church were invaded in 1864 by Union troops who were advancing north to capture Spanish Fort and Blakeley, strongholds protecting Mobile. They were given permission to camp at the church and on the grounds. The Howards helped serve the soldiers, and Daphne was among those cooking for the men. She would have been nearly sixty years old at this point. After the war, Daphne's life was virtually unchanged. She continued to live at the hotel, and she still attended the Methodist church, sitting in the balcony and singing her heart out. When she died, her funeral was held at the church, and she was buried in the only integrated cemetery at that time: the Stokes family plot.

When the first post office was established in Daphne, a name was needed. Mrs. Howard asked her husband, who became the first postmaster, to name the town in honor of her dear friend, so the name of Daphne was given to the lovely Eastern Shore town.

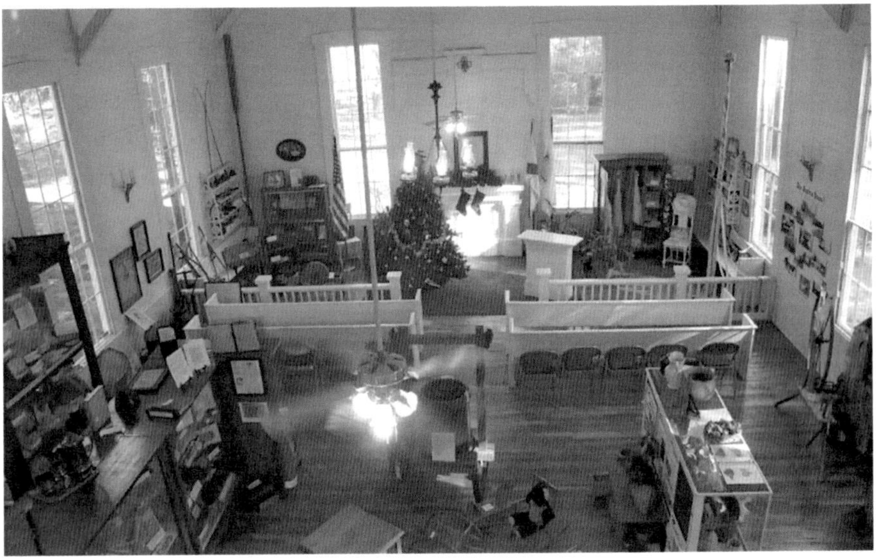

A view of Daphne Methodist Church Museum from the slave gallery. *Photo by Penny H. Taylor.*

Parishioners of the church missed her voice coming from the balcony—at least, some missed it. Others said that she could still be heard during the singing of the hymns. Sometimes when the altar guild was inside the sanctuary cleaning and preparing for the Sunday worship services, members would be serenaded by lovely spiritual humming sounds coming from the rafters of the church. The Daphne Methodist Church building was the home of the active congregation until it built a new sanctuary. Then the old one was in danger of being lost. It was used for community meetings until a devastating hurricane nearly destroyed the historic building. The City of Daphne stepped in and leased the building to house its artifact collection. The City of Daphne Museum was opened in 2001; it preserves the heritage of the church and of the "Jubilee City." When the timing is right, humming can be heard coming from the balcony. Those who hear it say that it might be the wind, but it also might be a deep female voice, somewhat distorted. The tunes are not always discernable, but one witness said that it was the hymn "Swing Low, Sweet Chariot."

Daphne Methodist Church Museum is located at 405 Dryer Avenue, Daphne, Alabama, and is open Friday, Saturday and Sunday afternoons. The website can be found at www.daphnemuseumalabama.org. Another note must be added. The nearby Stokes family cemetery is a favorite location for ghost hunters. Daphne's grave is unmarked, but one there is designated as "Mammy," the family servant of the Stokes family.

THE BRIDE OF THE BRANCH: YANCEY BRANCH, DAPHNE

In the olden days, before there were very many buildings or even roads, the waterways were the main points of reference for any place in Baldwin County. Freshwater streams and rivers flowing into Mobile Bay were bountiful in Daphne (the Village). In fact, there was a thriving business of selling fresh spring water to oceangoing vessels that came to Daphne specifically for that purpose.

D'Olive Creek, Rock Creek and Fly Creek are the main waterways entering the bay in this area, but numerous small branches flow into those creeks. One of those was the place of a dramatic event that still reverberates on its banks. Yancey Branch was named for one of the survivors of the Battle of Fort Mims. In 1813, William R. Yancey's mother is credited with pulling apart a section of the blockade and slipping into the woods with two children: her ten-year-old son and the small daughter of her slave, who had already been taken into captivity by the Creek Indians. She fled south to the new town of Blakeley, where she knew that her friends, the Earle family, had located. She stayed with them for a while and then heard that there were opportunities for work farther south at the Village.

Andrew Jackson was soon ordered to the southern shores to defeat the Creeks and settle all disputes for the lands there. The cry "Remember Fort Mims" was heard throughout the South, and William responded. Having witnessed the brutal murder of friends and family, he was determined to do his part. He was too young to become a soldier, but Jackson agreed to let him be a drummer. William was present when General Jackson spoke to his troops from a branch of an oak tree just before the army left for the Battle of New Orleans. William fought alongside those who ultimately won that famous battle. After the war, many soldiers were awarded land in payment for their services, and William was granted land near the Village. He and his mother built a family home on the banks of the little creek that came to be named Yancey Branch.

Yancey Branch was located along the Old Spanish Trail, which connected the landings at the Village to Pensacola by wagons or stagecoaches that crossed the branch by means of a wooden bridge. Yancey Bridge was a common meeting place for exchange of goods from farms and towns to the east. It was here at this bridge that the Yancey family established a small farm and were able to earn a meager living providing services to those traders meeting there. They maintained the simple wooden bridge, often having to repair it after torrential rains caused the branch to overflow. Even in normal spells, Yancey Branch was known for its boggy patches of mud of such consistency that locals called it quicksand, and during the rains they were deadly. It is here at the spot where the old bridge crossed the boggy branch that the Bride of the Branch seeks the man to whom she had pledged her love.

Lockwood Plantation was one of the few large farms operating in the area in the early 1800s. John Lockwood grew cotton on thousands of acres just east of Yancey Branch. He sold his cotton to a broker who met him at the exchange point at Yancey Bridge. One of the wagon drivers and bay ferrymen, Joshua, made the regular run. Lockwood often let his lovely daughter accompany his men to the Yancey place. When Joshua and Janine first saw each other, it was love at first sight. Lovely Janine began to contrive ways to meet Joshua there as often as possible, and their love grew.

Mr. Lockwood had a dark, sinister secret. He was a gambler, and as is true with many who are victims of the addiction, he was soon in debt. Unbeknownst to his family, he had already lost the plantation, and in determination to win it back, he went once again to the tavern near the bay to try his luck. A wealthy doctor from Mobile who was widowed had already become enamored of Lockwood's beautiful daughter, but she scorned his advances. The doctor schemed a wicked plan. He bought drinks for Lockwood until the plantation owner was far from sober. The card game built to a climactic finale, when Lockwood had nothing else to wager. The doctor suggested that he would consider the lovely Janine as a prize for the final hand. Of course, the doctor walked away with the promise of marriage to the prize he coveted. Lockwood had reached the lowest point in his life but knew that he was honor bound to meet his debts. When he told his daughter of her future, she wept and pleaded, but all to no avail. Arrangements were made for her to be ready for her future husband the next day. She was dressed in her wedding gown and veil when the doctor came to fetch her; her trousseau was packed in trunks loaded on the wagon. Janine sat bravely in the wagon as she met her fate. Some wondered at her bearing that day, not knowing that she had written a missive to her lover with plans for an escape.

The night came early as the rains started to fall. The wind picked up speed, and the torrents of water seemed to blind the doctor and the bride as they approached Yancey Branch. The roads near the bridge were rapidly becoming a muddy quagmire. As the doctor's wagon crossed the wooden bridge, he was unaware that the lover lay in wait, masked as a highwayman. Just as the wagon reached the opposite bank, Joshua sprang from his hiding place and called for the doctor to halt. The doctor drew his pistol and took aim at Joshua, hitting his mark. The horses bolted at the shot and reared in such a manner as to upset the wagon and throw the passengers into the road. The doctor was caught under the wheels of the wagon, but the bride jumped to safety and began to run to Joshua. As she headed toward her wounded love, she started to sink. It was dark and wet, and she had run into the muddy abyss of quicksand. The ground seemed solid enough to support her slight frame, but the angry mud there reached up and began to pull her under. She began screaming, "Joshhhhhuuuaaaa!"

She cried out, but he was wounded and unconscious. Eventually, the rain washed his face and helped him regain his senses. He saw the doctor lifeless under the wagon and heard his love calling his name. He pulled himself toward the sound of her voice but searched in vain for her. He refused to leave the branch and continued his search for days and then weeks that stretched into months and years. He was seen with a lantern every night walking the banks of the branch, calling for Janine. He kept his vigil because he heard her calling his name night after night. "Joshuaaaaa…" One morning, Joshua's lantern was found abandoned beside the quicksand pit. It was assumed that he, too, had accidentally stepped into the mud and disappeared. Others believed that he had purposefully joined his love at last.

Mr. Lockwood continued to search for his precious daughter. His punishment was a long life in which to repent his sins. Mrs. Yancey was the first to see signs of the Bride of the Branch. One evening at dusk, she saw a light at the edge of the stream. It was swinging to and fro. As she walked on the opposite side of the branch, she began to make out the form of a lovely young lady dressed in a white wedding gown. As she watched, the girl began to sink into the quicksand, all the time calling for "Josssshhhuuuaaa."

During the night hours, especially during heavy rainfall, the sounds of Janine calling for her love are often heard. The original bridge is gone and the road is no longer there, but the branch still flows. It can be seen well from the pedestrian trail along Whispering Pines Road, a wooden bridge. Maybe it is the sound of the rushing waters that creates the voice calling for help. Many hear it still today, and sometimes the Bride of the Branch is seen by those who believe. Beware the quicksand if you want a closer look.

THE VILLAGE VISITORS: VILLAGE POINT PARK PRESERVE, DAPHNE

The City of Daphne has done an amazing job preserving those historic sites that first put Daphne on the map. Village Point Park Preserve has bay-front access with a pier and sandy beach, a pavilion and walking trails that pass two significant spots. One is the D'Olive (dough-leave) cemetery, and the other is Jackson's Oak. The city has also constructed a fantastic boardwalk, which crosses D'Olive Creek and connects with the Eastern Shore Trail. It has been lovingly nicknamed "Gator Alley" because of the numerous alligators visible from the walkway. Visitors to these two parks are frequently met with evidence of hauntings.

Village Point is located where the earliest town (the Village) was located on the Eastern Shore of Mobile Bay at an Indian fish camp named "Neutral Ground." Dominique D'Olive had interests in the Village and is considered

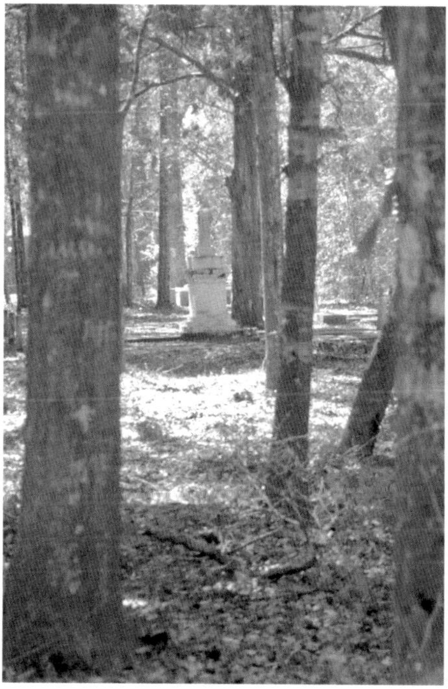

The D'Olive family cemetery, Village Point Preserve, Daphne. *Photo by Penny H. Taylor.*

one of the founding fathers of the settlement. The area changed hands as the European countries fought for control in the New World. In 1787, when the county was a part of Spanish West Florida, Louis D'Olive, a son of Dominique, was granted an eight-hundred-arpen (about eight hundred acres) Spanish land grant and came to the Village to build a home for his family. He developed a hotel, which he named La Belle Rose, and purchased thousands of additional acres, where he raised livestock. The family cemetery marks the graves of members of the family who lived and died here. One of the daughters, Louisa, married Major Lewis Stark, who owned a brickworks factory that furnished some of the bricks to build Fort Morgan. Louisa and Major Stark are also buried in the family cemetery.

Many reports of encounters at the cemetery are documented. One prominent businessman and his son were visiting there and snapped a photo with a phone. The image of a man in colonial garb is clear in the photo, which is unfortunately of a very low resolution yet nonetheless extremely convincing. Several groups of investigators have gone there at night and obtained readings after calling to the family in French.

The cemetery is not the only haunted spot in the park. The Jackson's Oak is named for the famous Andrew Jackson, who addressed his men there as they prepared to march to the Battle of New Orleans in the War of 1812.

A historic marker on Highway 98 reads as follows:

> *Standing on a low limb of a giant oak tree near here, General Andrew Jackson made a pep talk to his troops, fresh from their victory at the Battle of Horse Shoe Bend and poised before advancing on the British and Spanish at Pensacola, and the British at New Orleans.*

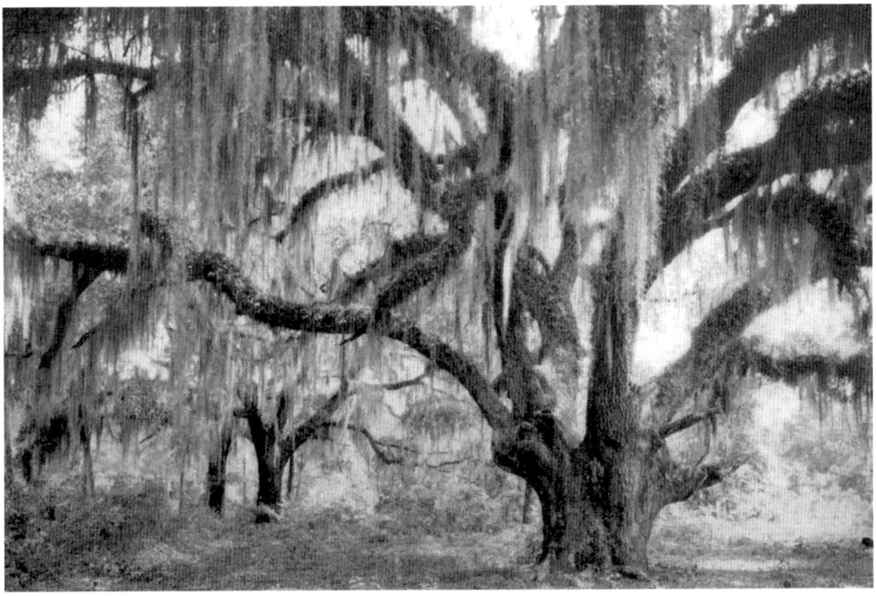

Here from the branches of an oak tree, Andrew Jackson rallied his troops before marching to fight the Battle of New Orleans during the War of 1812. Jackson's Oak is in the Village Point Preserve, Daphne. *Author's collection.*

> *Victories in all these battles speaks well for the rest his men enjoyed here, as well as the talk.*
>
> *Probably the only occasion in Jackson's long career that he was on a low limb.*

Experiences near the tree have mainly included orbs, but some investigators report the wind whistling through the branches on even the stillest of nights. Andrew Jackson has been known to make other appearances as well. Many people have seen a soldier in a War of 1812 uniform riding on a white horse in the middle of both D'Olive Creek and Yancey Branch.

A walk in the park can take one through the stories of settlers and soldiers who are all still there. There are also reports of experiences with Native Americans along the shoreline. One lady was having a drink at a place near the bay. She looked into the mirror behind the bar and saw an Indian dressed only in a breechcloth standing behind her. He had a headband with a string of beads and feathers hanging down almost to his waist. The lady turned around to talk to this person, whom she assumed was in costume for some party nearby. There was no one there. Looking again at the mirror, she saw his reflection start to fade away. She quickly called the bartender to witness the apparition, but by the time he got there and she pointed out the spot on the mirror, the Indian had completely disappeared. Well, maybe not completely. The mirror had a cloudy spot that could not be wiped away. The mirror had no reflective qualities at that spot. No one could remember if the mirror had that spot before this incident, but it certainly did afterward. The misty mirror stayed that way, and many a night the story was told to customers by the bartender. It was still there when the building burned to the ground. All along the bay near Bayfront Park were camps where Indians came to gather and dry seafood for their winter stores. Perhaps one of them stayed when the rest of the clan went home.

Jubilee Point Park Preserve is located on Highway 98 or Main Street, Daphne, north of downtown Daphne. www.villagepointpark.com.

MASONIC HALL GUARDIAN: OLD DAPHNE MASONIC HALL

On the Old Spanish Trail in Daphne there stands an eerie stucco building. It was once a Masonic Lodge and later was used as housing and as the police station for the city. Throughout its colorful history, people have had strange encounters there and in the woods that surround it.

All the secret rites of the Masonic order would naturally make the lodge a perfect house for spirits, but the site of the building was haunted even before it was constructed. The old Masonic Lodge in Daphne was built near Yancey Branch on the Old Spanish Trail, the major thoroughfare of the day. There were quite a few homes all along the trail. A nearby well was shared by several families in the community. It is common knowledge that at news of approaching Union soldiers, the residents along the Branch hid silver, gold and jewelry in the well.

There are those who say that they see fireballs flying up and down the street that is now the remnants of the ancient byway. They described them as brimstone orbs that seemed to be hurled with great strength. Most people say the fireballs are really the shots fired here in a skirmish during the War Between the States. Here a troop of Union soldiers transporting munitions was attacked by a small contingency of guerrilla Confederate soldiers. There were several killed and more wounded before the Union was driven away.

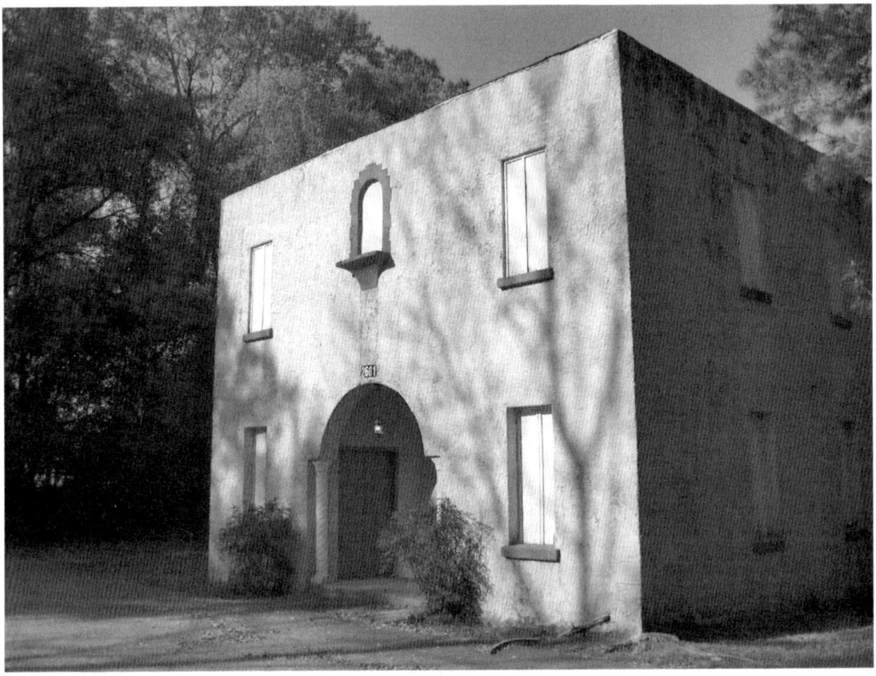

Old Masonic Hall, Old Spanish Trace, Daphne. *Photo by Ken Balme.*

The injured Confederates were taken to a makeshift hospital at "Uncle Johnny's" house in Daphne on the bay, but one Confederate soldier had suffered a bullet to the head and was left for dead. Upon reviving from his unconscious state, the soldier stumbled into the woods, where he came upon the well. Here he met some women and children who immediately began to care for him and give him fresh water to drink. The soldier was not able to speak or hear and seemed to be in a state of shock.

The women and children at the well heard horses and wagons approaching, which was actually the munitions company returning. They ran into the nearby woods and motioned for the young Confederate to follow them. The young man seemed unable to hear or speak as the Union troops came into the clearing. The Union major called to the soldier to halt, but the young soldier simply turned and started walking away. After firing warning shots, the major took aim and shot the soldier in the back. The major approached the body and turned him over to see his face. He was terror-struck, for the young soldier was his brother. Just at that moment, the Confederate forces returned and the Union contingency fled. The women and children came out of the woods, dragged the Confederate's body and hid it until they could return safely at night. When they came to bury the body, it was nowhere to be found. To this day, no one can explain the disappearance of the body, but the sightings in the area keep the story alive. Some say that they can hear the rumblings of wagons and the hooves of horses. The apparition of the young soldier has been witnessed by enough people that his presence is common knowledge. Some say he is guarding the treasure hidden in the well.

Author and historian Joan White Crowder had a personal experience with the sightings, as she wrote in her wonderful book *Tell It to an Old Hollow Log*. During World War II, she and her family lived in the two-story Masonic Lodge building. She vividly recalled the uneasy feelings her family experienced while living there. Several incidents made them aware that there may have been other presences in the building. There was water running, steps sounding and even the disappearance of Joan's clothing from her closet. Her grandparents, living upstairs, had an unpleasant personal encounter with the spirit that was frightening. Her grandmother's recitation of the Lord's Prayer and her grandfather's confrontation with the presence brought a tenuous compatibility with the ghost. Joan related that the family still had some experiences in the house but that because her grandparents and the ghost had reached a mutual understanding, the family began to laugh about the tricks played on them.

Later, the building housed the Daphne Police Department. The officers and staff working in the building were reluctant to relate their experiences there, but tales continued to abound about the happenings taking place. People outside still noticed strange occurrences, as fireballs would be seen flying up and down the street and in the nearby woods. Several staff members did not like being in the building alone and refused to work late hours on occasion. There were the same sounds that were reported by the former residents: stomping feet upstairs and water flowing from spigots in the kitchen area. They believed.

A Fair Hope of Hauntings: Fairhope

The city of Fairhope was founded on the theory of the "Single Tax Colony" and has a colorful history going back to its founding in 1894. The Single Tax Colony Cemetery is noted as a favorite of paranormal specialists, and there are several houses that are haunted. It seems that the free spirit environment welcomes all who come, alive or not. One could spend all day (or night) in the Fairhope City Museum and never be alone. There are always activities in the old building, whether the museum is open or not. Director Donnie Barrett is a walking encyclopedia of all things past and present. He is an expert on every subject imaginable, except that he does not know who keeps making noises and appearances in the former city hall.

The building was constructed for the city government in 1928 by Oswalt Forester using Clay City Tile. It housed the mayor, the police department, the fire department, the city council chambers and the city clerk. As additional buildings were constructed over the years, all of the offices except those of the police department moved to new facilities. The police department was headquartered there, and the jail was in use until 2001. In later years, the old jail cells were used mainly as holding cells during processing, and longer-term prisoners were housed in a more modern cellblock built to the rear of the station. Fairhope wisely saved the building and converted it to a city museum, which has become the focal point of all things past in Fairhope thanks to the foresight of the director, the mayor and council and countless volunteers who care about preservation of the heritage of this unique city. The museum today replicates the original use of the spaces but has displays covering every aspect of the town's history. Everything is extremely well presented, and the museum has become a repository for all things of value—including those spirits that want to be heard and felt.

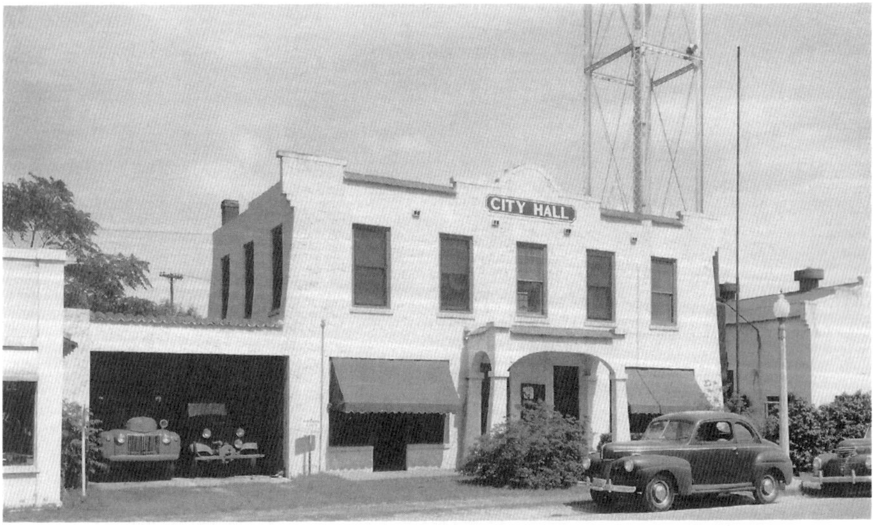

Old Fairhope City Hall and Jail were built in 1928. *Courtesy of Fairhope City Museum.*

The director has had personal experiences that he cannot explain. Once he was at the top of the stairs writing on a clipboard and heard someone's footsteps coming up the stairs toward him. When they reached the top, he turned to greet the guest, but no one was there. He has heard the jail door slam shut several times when he has been alone, but every time that he went down to check to be sure no one was in the building, he found both cell doors standing open.

Three ladies who love to search for ghosts have amazing stories to share. Sherri got permission to go to the jail one night with her recording equipment. She asked if anyone was there with her, and she heard and felt a powerful *swish* go right past

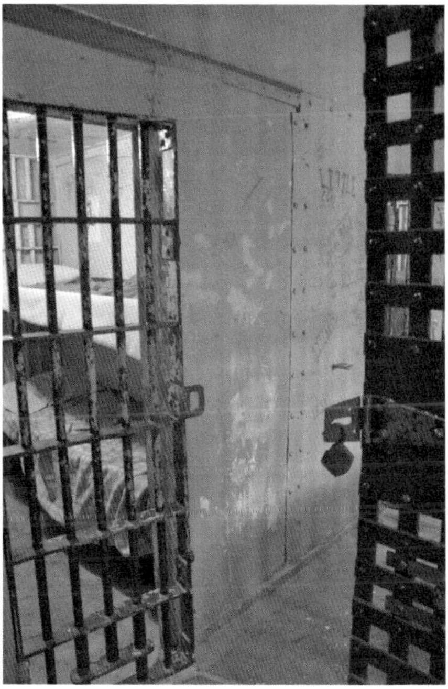

The old original jail cells in Fairhope Jail, now the Fairhope Museum. *Photo by Penny Taylor.*

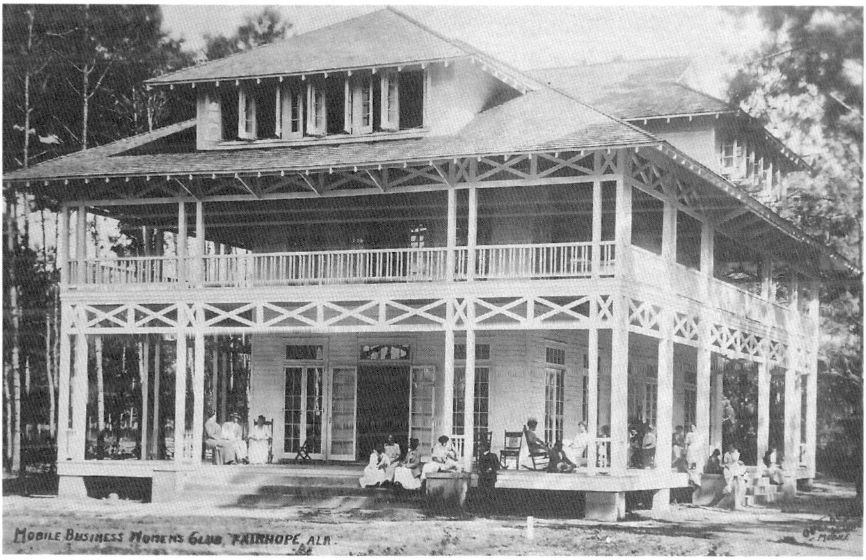

Pine Needles, a Fairhope Bayfront retreat built by the Mobile Business Women's Club. *Courtesy of Fairhope Museum.*

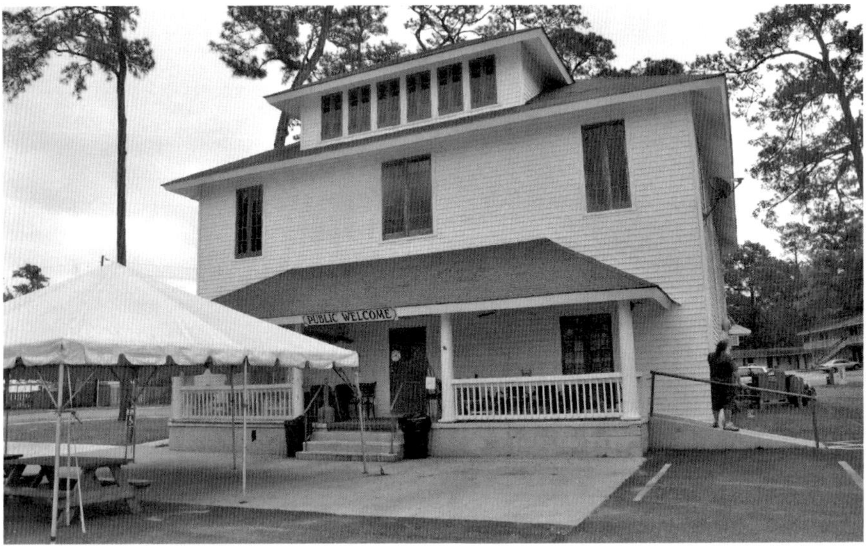

American Legion Hall Post 199, once the Pine Needles Women's Retreat, Fairhope. *Photo by Penny H. Taylor.*

her ear. When she listened to the EVP later, she distinctly heard, "Cannabis high." A wind came out of the cell and blew right into her face.

Another highly inhabited building is the American Legion Post 199, built in 1912. It was originally a retreat facing the bay built by the Mobile Business Women's Club, which named it Pine Needles. It was later rented out as residences and offices, and for a few years boxing matches were held in the third-floor room. The American Legion Post 199 took over in 1961, when the porches were enclosed to enlarge the interior space. Those who believe are certain that there are several inhabitants of the old place. Loud bumping sounds are heard from the third floor, and lights are seen in that loft even though there is no electricity there. When Sherri and her team of investigators spent an evening there, they were met with encouraging greetings. When the investigator asked if the unseen beings were upset that the retreat had become a bar, the answer was clearly recorded: "No, I love it." When asked if it was acceptable that women were served drinks at the bar, the answer, however, was "No." There are waitresses who refuse to work alone there, often reporting glasses being overturned and the unexplained movement of objects. Sometimes, water is heard running through the pipes. One woman even said that she has heard the sound of a broom sweeping the floor. That sounds like a housemother, right? I wonder if she ever encounters the boxer on the third floor.

PART III

THE GRAND HOTEL

People have been coming to Point Clear for rest and relaxation since the 1830s, when the first hotel was built. It is an icon in the county, a most consistent presence throughout the history of the county. Its moss-covered oaks, bay-front view, excellent dining and most gracious guest rooms make up a campus that has been the setting for thousands of memories. The powerful existence of those memories lends itself to hauntings. Many guests have seen the 1850s owner coming down the grand staircase smoking his pipe. Servers swear that silverware is knocked to the floor if not put out correctly. Some guests say that they have seen a World War II soldier wearing no shoes walking down the hallway of the oldest building. In fact, soldiers in training there during the war did indeed remove their shoes to protect the floors and honor the elegance of the hotel. There are some hauntings that deserve to be told in detail, so come sit on the porch and hear them.

THE GRAND PIANO MAN: JACK NORMAND

The Grand Hotel at Point Clear has always been called simply "the Hotel"—not the Grand, as is sometimes heard today among the younger generation. Old folks know it only as the Hotel. This is because it is the quintessential image of a hotel that holds the past as well as the future within its walls. It is one of those places where the past and the present often merge. The Hotel has been around for years, as early as the first people to come to the Eastern Shore for the cool breezes in the summer that blew away the fear of yellow fever and the salt water that enhanced the health of the body. Guests who come to the Hotel for a stay today experience the same feeling of timelessness that people have felt from its inception. Today, guests may swim, dine and dance to the music of the grand piano in the dining room. But those who hear the grand piano playing in the middle of the night long after the dining room has closed are hearing the resonance of lives from the past.

Actually, the hotel is what is now called a "return destination." It is a standard summer getaway for many guests who are a part of the heritage of the hotel; they look forward to the time of relaxation and to seeing old friends as they once again walk the lovely grounds, play golf, ride bicycles, watch the sunset and enjoy evening meals in the main dining room. They remember when only those young men under twelve were excused from wearing a tie, and they remember the band. Sarah and her family, from Pine Bluff, spent two weeks there each summer. She swam in the hotel pool, enjoyed the activities led by the staff and donned a party dress each night for the family dinner, where she especially enjoyed the band and the bandleader, Jack Normand. He would greet her by name upon her return each year, and she remembered standing near him for at least one song while her parents danced. After dinner, the band often moved out to Julep Point, a terrazzo tile open-air dance floor, where couples danced under the stars. Those stars over Mobile Bay inspired Jack to create his signature medley for "Stars Fell on Alabama" and "On Mobile Bay," which was always the band's final tune of the evening. Even after the band packed up instruments and headed home, the strains of the tune seemed to be a part of the salty breezes that blew gently across the hotel grounds. Those sounds have actually never disappeared.

Sarah was only one of those guests who grew up under the eyes of the bandleader who held the rhythm of the hotel in his fingertips. His music and personality inspired many guests to write notes or letters thanking him. He kept those missives from his more than forty-year stint as the "Music Man" of the hotel, taking joy in knowing that he had helped make memories for so many people. But that love of sharing music did not die with him in 1990. He continues to treat guests to the sounds he shared throughout his life. Sarah is one of those guests who wrote him a

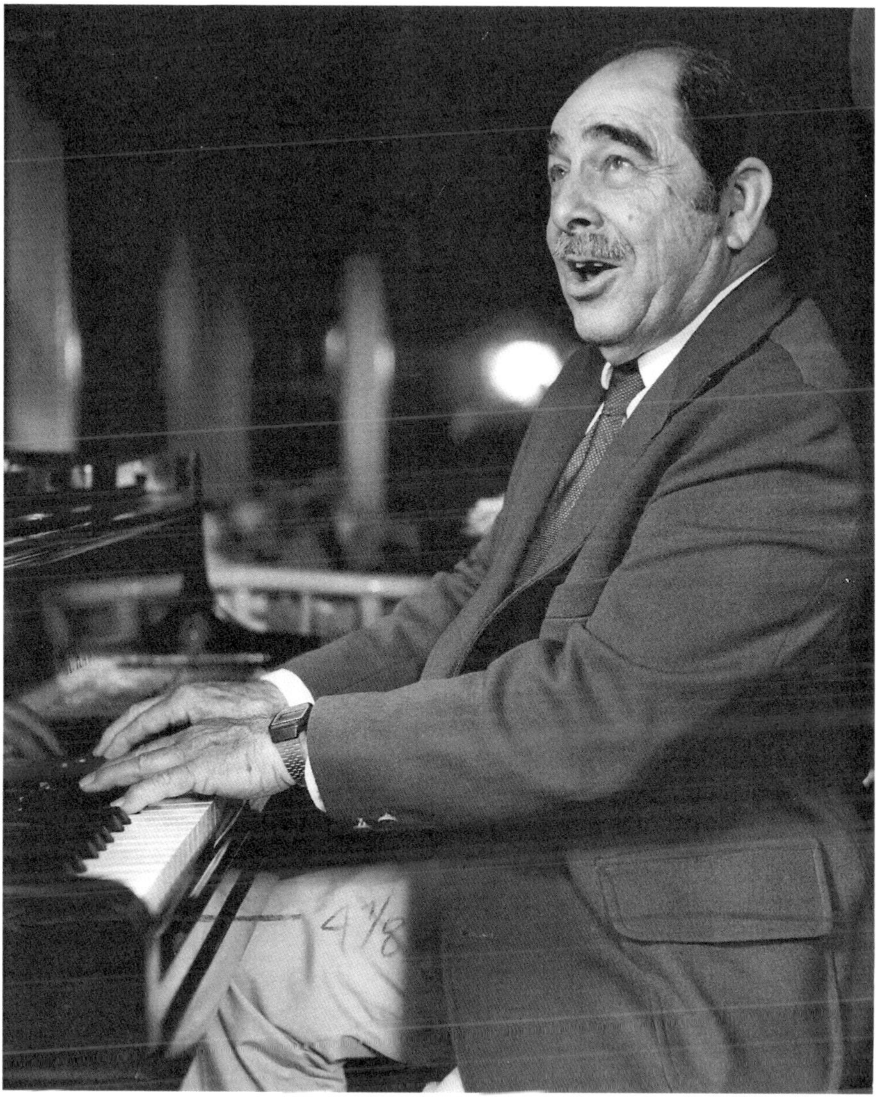

Bandleader Jack Normand at the piano, Grand Hotel. *Courtesy of Robert Normand.*

thank-you note, returned as an adult and now is among those who can hear his music at the hotel long after dining and dancing hours are over.

Jack's life began in Bunky, Louisiana, but his professional life began in New Orleans, where the streets were full of the music that moved him. His mother insisted that he have piano lessons, but that was the extent of his formal training. Yet he had that innate sense of rhythm and true love for boogie-woogie sounds. During the Depression, he and a friend were working at a grocery store in the Big Easy for fifty cents per week, from dawn 'til dusk. One night, they got a job to play at a honky-tonk. They played the only three songs they knew, over and over, but were awarded five dollars each. From then on, they became professional musicians, leaving the days of grocery stores forever. He was popular in New Orleans and was known as a big little band, as members of the band could play so many different instruments and a tremendous variety of tunes. His music was always flavored by his Cajun heritage, of which he was justly proud.

He was playing at the Fountain Lounge of the Roosevelt Hotel in New Orleans when the owner of the newly remodeled Grand Hotel, Ed Roberts, heard him play. He signed Jack's band to play for the reopening of the hotel on April 18, 1941. The band was so well liked that Roberts engaged him on a more long-term basis, but the world changed with the bombing of Pearl Harbor in December of that same year. Jack joined the Army Air Force, where he played bass drum with the Air Force Marching Band based at Maxwell Air Force Base in Montgomery.

After the war, he returned to his native New Orleans, where his band was engaged at some of the more prestigious hotels and lounges. He was playing at the Blue Room in the Roosevelt when he was persuaded to return to the Grand Hotel for a six-week gig. That gig turned into a lifetime. He loved the community of Fairhope and soon had his family entrenched there in a lovely old home overlooking Mobile Bay. He and his wife, Genevieve, had five children, whom they were determined to raise in a healthy atmosphere. All five of the children were musical and played with his band at points in his career. His wife was not a musician, he chuckled once, but she was a mighty fine Cajun cook! By 1976, two of his sons, Danny and Robert, were permanent "sidemen" in the trio, and Jack changed the name to the Normand Family Band. His other children—Glenn, Jeanine and Laurie—joined the group, each being able to play several instruments. Sometimes they would even switch instruments during a show. Jack would ask them, "Musical chairs?"

Everybody loved Jack. His charm was a part of the hospitality at the hotel. Jack was a master at the piano and, more so, a master at the heart. He played almost every night and for special events. He played for couples on their honeymoons, for couples returning to the Hotel for anniversaries, for birthdays and for every special date. He had an uncanny knack for remembering which tunes were special to guests, and when he noticed a returning couple come into the dining room, he often interrupted his set with the favorite song of that particular couple. No wonder he was so loved!

The band was known for its versatility. Jack loved the "oldies" of the big band era but could perform the latest hit numbers with equal finesse. His children, perhaps, kept him abreast of the newest trends on the hit parade. No matter what piece the band played, it was always "danceable." Toe tapping was always seen among the guests, and provision always had to be made for a dance floor. Jack was also an accomplished performer on the accordion, which he continued to play until he was in his eighties. Jack made two recordings and was featured nationally on several occasions. Paul Harvey paid the family a tribute in one of his broadcasts, calling them his "Musical Cajun Friends."

Marilyn is one of those guests who has fond memories of Jack. He played for her wedding night in 1976—he congratulated her and her new husband on their marriage, asking about a request from them. They were actually at a loss, and he immediately decided that "When a Man Loves a Woman" should be their song. His rendition of the Percy Sledge hit seemed to be written just for them, and when they returned to the hotel for anniversary dinners, he played their song, right up until he died. Marilyn swears that he did not stop even then.

Jack died in 1990, playing nearly to the end. People from all over the world mourned his passing and knew that the Hotel would never be the same. Many journalists and colleagues paid him tribute. In a memorial written by Joey Bunch for the *Mobile Press Register*, an interview with Bucky Miller seemed to summarize the feelings that all had for Jack. Bucky was another icon at the hotel, having worked there greeting guests for more than half a century. He told the reporter of the first time he heard Jack play. He was outside but went straight into the dining room and walked up to the band, saying, "Put me in the alley, man." This was New Orleans slang for playing the blues, and Jack did. "He could play them better than anybody I've ever heard and still could," Bucky said. Bucky emphasized that more than anything, however, Jack's friendship and manners best described him. "He was a true gentleman," Bucky said. "I tried to be like him."

Almost as soon as Jack died, guests began hearing the strands of his signature tune, "Stars Fell on Alabama" blended with "On Mobile Bay," played only as Jack could play. Marilyn and her husband went to the Hotel for their anniversary dinner the June after Jack died. The band was wonderful, but they missed Jack and mourned his passing with each tune they heard. After dinner, the couple took a stroll along the shoreline. They sat on the pier for a long time, even long after the dining room had closed. They began the slow, romantic walk back to their room, passing the dining room. They looked at each other in wonder, for both were hearing the same thing. They were hearing a piano playing "Stars Fell on Alabama." There did not seem to be any backup band, but the tune was clear as crystal to the couple. Marilyn's husband took her in his arms, and they danced a slow, nostalgic dance to the melody they were hearing. The piano notes rang clearly in the balmy air. Soon the tune blended to "On Mobile Bay," and the couple then knew that it was Jack playing his signature tune. The most beautiful part of the story is that as the signature tuned ended, the notes began to sound the melody of "When a Man Loves a Woman," until the melody disappeared into the night. The couple shared their story with their children and a few friends, but most just nodded with a tolerant smile. Every listener believed that this couple had heard the song in their hearts alone.

They were not the only ones to have heard Jack play late in the evening. Sarah returned to the hotel in the late 1990s to recuperate from an injury. She knew that she would find healing and restoration at the hotel of her childhood's happiest memories. She took a walk late at night, and she, too, heard Jack playing the piano on the terrace of Julep Point.

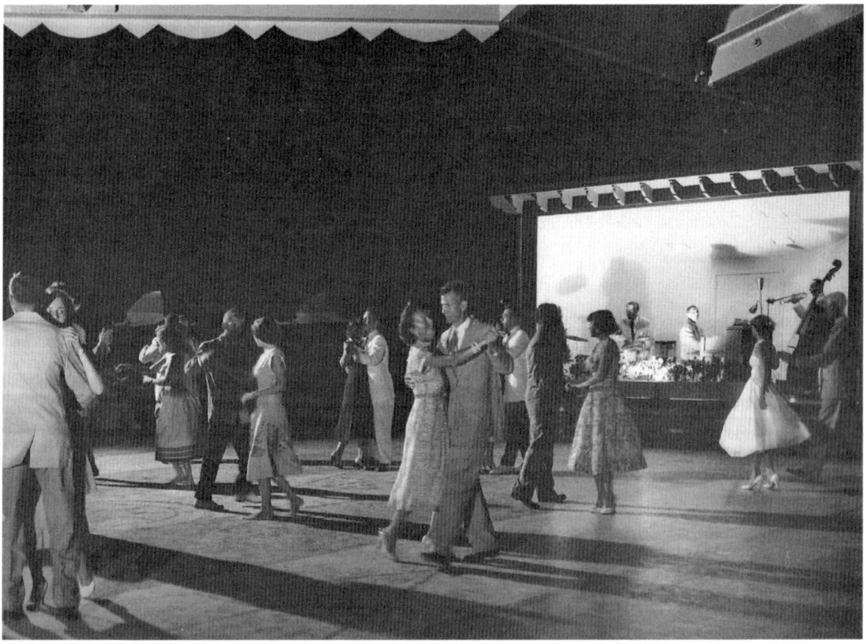

Dancing at Julep Point, Grand Hotel, circa 1960. *Courtesy of Grand Hotel.*

As she walked closer to the sound at the point, she saw a cloud of mist on the bandstand on the dark stage, but on the dance floor, she distinctly saw a swaying couple looking into each other's eyes. Sarah, who had loved to talk to Jack in her childhood, approached the stage only to see the band disappear and hear the sounds evaporate into the mist. One lady who heard the piano late at night asked another person on the lawn if they heard the sounds she was hearing. The other guest said, "Of course. The Hotel keeps the sound system playing tapes all night." The next morning, the guest asked the maître d' if that was true and was told that all was quiet during the night in the dining room. Those who believe can hear the Grand Piano Man at the Grand Hotel. You see, these songs call to those in love—those who are returning to the Hotel for the sake of remembrance. Those are the couples who go to dance to the music that perhaps only those in love can hear. Of course, they begin to dance on the grounds at the Hotel. Can you hear the music? It will go on until dawn.

Author's note: Unfortunately, since Hurricane Katrina, fewer guests have heard the sounds of the piano coming from the dining room. Perhaps the piano that was ruined held the magic. I know this much is true: Jack played on my wedding night in 1976, and in 1996 I heard his music for our twentieth anniversary in the dining room, late at night, at the hotel. We will return again every June until we can once again hear his magic.

A publication highlighting the ambience and outstanding recipes of the hotel is Grand Traditions, *published in 2009 by PCH Hotels and Resorts Inc., One Grand Boulevard, Point Clear, Alabama, 36564. ISBN 978-0-9822393-0-8.*

Black Magic: Confederate Rest Cemetery

Late evening golfers on the Lakewood Golf Course at the Grand Hotel tell of unusual sounds heard near the hole adjoining the Point Clear Cemetery. Neighbors and joggers even say that they have witnessed an apparition that tells the story of one of the soldiers buried there at Confederate Rest—the story of the bond that exists between man and horse.

Punta Clara has enticed visitors to the Eastern Shore of Mobile Bay since the earliest days of settlement in the southern part of the state. The

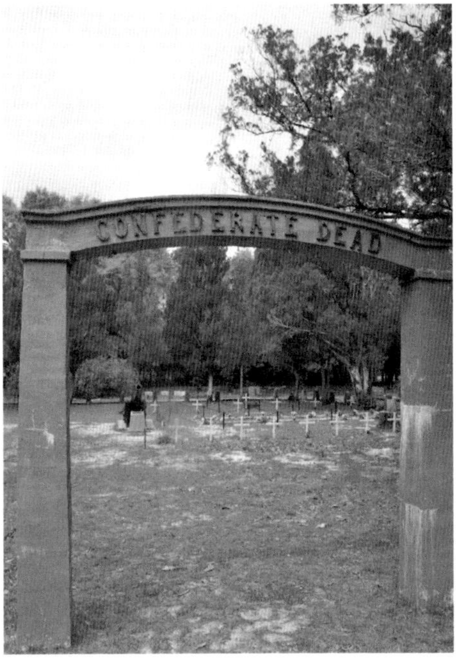

Confederate Rest Cemetery, Point Clear. Here are buried more than three hundred Confederates who died at the hospital housed at the Grand Hotel during the War Between the States. *Photo by Penny H. Taylor.*

hotel is set among many bay-front homes built by urbanites for escape from the summer heat of the cities. The first Grand Hotel existed in the 1830s but was destroyed by fire. It was replaced in 1847 by a grand two-story hotel built by W.H. Chamberlain. The forty-room hotel was used by the Confederate government to provide hospital care for the men wounded during the siege of Vicksburg, Mississippi. It was during this sad period that more than three hundred soldiers died and were buried in the nearby Confederate Rest.

The Siege of Vicksburg is one of the most horrifying accounts of the atrocities of war. For forty-seven days, citizens and soldiers were under fire from Union forces. Citizens and soldiers were victims of gunfire, disease and starvation. The descriptions of life there are heart-wrenching. People lived in caves carved in the sides of hills, and the ravages of hunger began to change the very nature of the people there. People were subsisting on rats and insects and were even chewing leather to try to gain some protein sustenance. Of course, this meant that mules and horses were often used as food. As the siege progressed, and the horses were underfed and starving, many were mercifully sacrificed as nourishment for others.

The story of Edmund Smith and his beloved horse is so powerful that the vestiges of the story are visible today. Edmund enlisted in the Confederate army and brought along his horse, Black Magic. He had raised Black Magic from a colt, trained him and worked his farm with him. Black Magic was much more than a workhorse; he was a racehorse as well. Edmund had begun earning acclaim for his horse throughout Missouri and even into Mississippi when the call for volunteers was heard in every town throughout the nation. Edmund left his parents, mounted his companion and headed for the battlefields. Members of Confederate cavalry usually had to provide their own horses, so when a man enlisted, he brought his horse with him, or one was donated to him by a Southern patriot.

He was one with his horse. Black Magic had saved Edmund's life on several occasions. They were sent to Vicksburg, a Confederate stronghold on the Mississippi River. Here they joined citizens and soldiers in enduring one of the most horrific experiences ever known. When hunger became the motivation for human behavior, Edmund was one of the few who would rather have died himself than see his beloved horse sacrificed. Black Magic had a soul that Edmund understood. He knew there was something really special about this horse. One night, while most were in a fitful sleep between bombardments from Union cannons, Edmund slipped to the river. He had a long talk with Black Magic and convinced the horse to run for his life. With a loving slap on the flank, he bid goodbye to half of his soul.

Black Magic somehow evaded capture by the Union forces and stayed hidden in the woods near Vicksburg. He saw the Confederacy finally surrender on July 4, 1863. Later, he witnessed Edmund among those who were sent by boat to the Point Clear hospital. Black Magic followed on the shoreline as the boat traveled down the Mississippi River to the Gulf of Mexico and then eastward. In some mystical fashion, he was able to arrive at the Grand Hotel in Point Clear as his master was being carried on a stretcher into the makeshift hospital. The hospital was under the guard of the Twenty-first Alabama Infantry, which was stationed at the Tam Denton Plantation nearby.

Black Magic was almost like a phantom horse even when he was alive. He could slip quietly in and out of places as if he were not even real. He came to the open window of the ward where Edmund lay dying. Edmund reached his wounded hand to touch the horse and died peacefully, knowing that Black Magic had escaped the brutalities of the war. Tragically, more than three hundred brave young men died there and were buried by the Twenty-first Alabama Infantry in a cemetery near the hotel in a trench grave. Most were not honored with a headstone at the time of the burials, and the records of the dead are now missing. They were lost in a fire, but a copy was supposed to have been rolled up and placed in the attic of the Point Clear Library. That record cannot be found today.

The members of the Twenty-first Alabama Infantry became attached to the loyal horse and sought to care for him as much as the horse would allow. They put meager rations out where he could find them, sometimes catching a glimpse of him in the forests near the trench graves. Men may not have known where Edmund was buried, but Black Magic did. The elusive horse was seen coming to the cemetery every evening right after dark. He would paw the ground and whinny a forlorn call to his master, never allowing anyone near him. He was seen for a few years after the war ended until one morning, when the horse was found dead in the cemetery, most think from grief. One member of the Twenty-first was determined that the two souls would be together. He buried the horse in the cemetery.

Soon after that, the locals began to once again hear the whinnies of a mourning horse, and occasionally someone would see him run through the cemetery. Often the ground near the graves was churned as if it had been pawed by hooves. Paranormal groups have spent nights there in the cemetery to try to detect presences, but for the most part, their readings are positive communications. One has reported sighting a Confederate soldier sitting in a tree. Members of the Twenty-first Alabama Infantry Reenactment group, however, have had encounters with Black Magic. They and the members of the local chapters of the Military Order of Stars and Bars organization have spent countless hours in the cemetery. The cannons, the entrance gate and the grave sites are respectfully tended and marked with flowers on

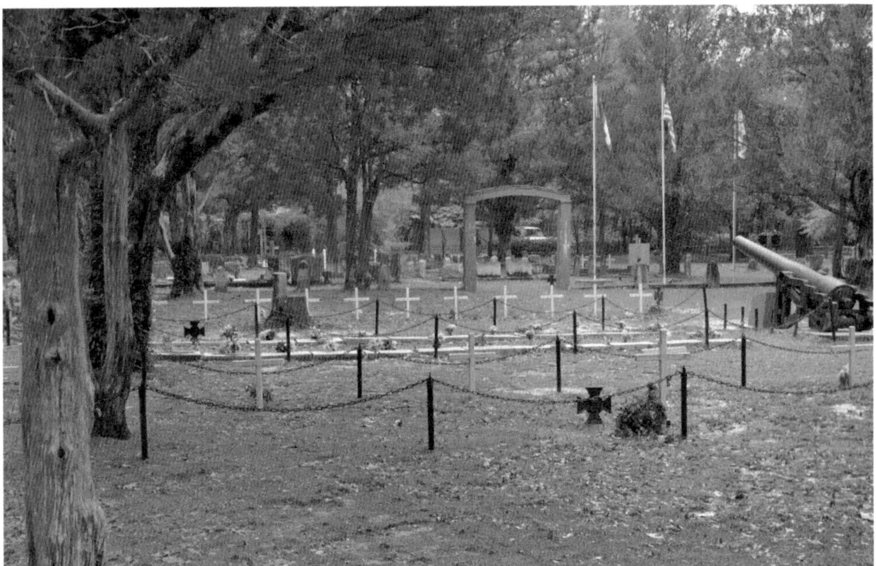

Most Confederates who died and were buried in trenches here at Confederate Rest had been wounded at Vicksburg. *Photo by Penny H. Taylor.*

Confederate Memorial Day. Thanks to these groups, many headstones now mark the graves of the known dead. Several of the members have heard the neighing of a horse nearby. One even heard horse hooves gallop through the cemetery. When ceremonies are held there, spectators often think that one of the reenactors has brought along his magnificent black stallion, for Black Magic is usually there near the edge of the woods.

The Confederate Rest Cemetery is a part of the Point Clear Cemetery located on Confederate Rest Road, just off Scenic Highway 98 in Point Clear, Alabama.

The *Ocean Wave*: Bay Boat Disaster, Point Clear

Sally Jane was working at the desk on a typical summer afternoon at the Grand Hotel. She looked up to see the excited faces of two children who exclaimed that they had seen the fireworks display right about sunset over the bay. Sally Jane looked puzzled and told them that she did not know what they had witnessed but that the hotel had not planned a fireworks display for that evening. She even called the concierge to be sure. The parents of the children assured Sally Jane that their entire family had watched the show, which lasted about five minutes. They did say that it was strange that they did not hear any loud booms or sounds usually associated with pyrotechnics. Sally Jane suggested that perhaps some boat offshore had shot some fireworks, and the family agreed that was probably the case. When Sally Jane began to ask if anyone else had similar reports, she found out that a few other employees had been told that a large light show was occasionally seen from the shores of the bay. Curious, Sally searched for clues about what this might have been and came across reports of a terrible bay boat explosion that had occurred at the hotel in 1871. She felt certain that this boat's traumatic and explosive demise must surely have left residual traces visible today.

The *Ocean Wave* was a bay boat, a boat designed with a shallow draft to ply the waters of Mobile Bay. Bay boats were steam-powered paddle wheelers that could accommodate hundreds of passengers and cargo as well. Many such boats made runs between Mobile and Pensacola, with dockings in between. Every hotel and town had a wharf extending out to the deeper waters. The busiest times for the boats were in the early summer, when many families in Mobile loaded up their clothing, food stores and sometimes even livestock for the annual trip to spend the summer on the shores of the bay. The Fish, Magnolia and Bon Secour Rivers were also summer destinations, complete with fishing and rowboat excursions. Magnolia Springs boasted quite a number of exclusive resort hotels and rustic getaway hostels all along its shore. The Cold Pond at the head of the river was a favorite swimming hole.

In the late 1800s, several bay boat companies began offering excursion outings. Such was the case with the twenty-seven-ton, ill-fated *Ocean Wave*. At the foot of Government Street in Mobile, the boat boarded about two hundred Sunday guests for a trip to Magnolia River, Fish River and Point Clear. This was one of the more affordable sightseeing excursions offered, and the *Ocean Wave* was probably carrying more passengers than it should have been. One family on the outing was that of G. Nicholas, who wanted to show his children where some of their Creole relatives lived on the banks of Weeks Bay. After a perfectly lovely outing, the final late afternoon stop was at Point Clear. The *Ocean Wave* docked at the end of the hotel pier, and guests spent a while having tea and walking the oak-covered pathways. Perhaps some even made a little stop at the Texas, a separate building that served as the bar for the hotel. No one could have known that a disaster was imminent.

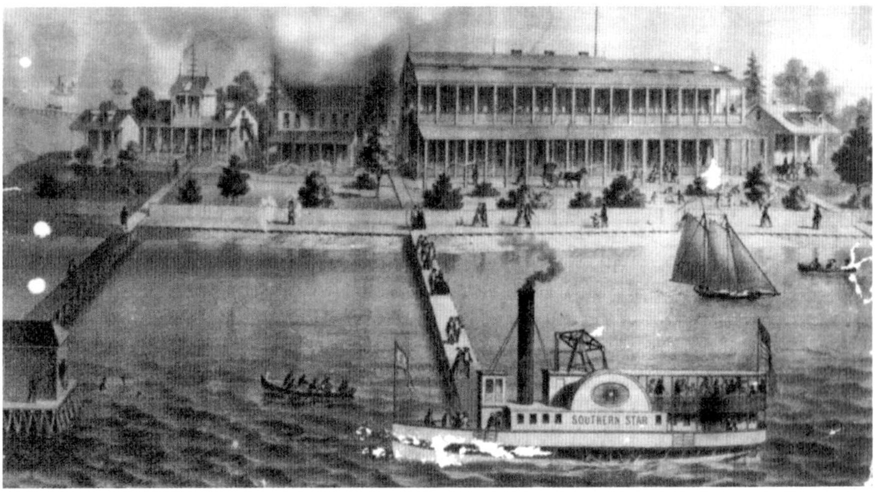

The Grand Hotel in 1871. The *Annie*, pictured here, burned just shortly before the great *Ocean Wave* explosion. *Courtesy of Bob Glennon.*

The hotel was filled to capacity, as this was in August 1871. It had recently reopened after a fire in 1869, and guests were once again relishing the bay breezes as they sat on the porches. One guest was Ben Lane, who gave the *Mobile Press Register* an eyewitness account of the explosion of the *Ocean Wave*. He had survived the War Between the States and enjoyed his visits to the hotel. He sometimes met his comrades, including the famous Admiral Raphael Semmes, who lived nearby and spent many afternoons on the porch of the hotel. On that Sunday, August 27, Ben watched the passengers walk up the pier to the hotel, chatted with several of them and then saw them return when the whistle sounded at 5:30 p.m. As soon as the boat pulled anchor, the boiler exploded with such force that clouds of smoke were visible miles away. Ben reported that he had been witness to many horrible atrocities during the war, but the disaster he saw at Point Clear was more heart-rending than any he had ever seen. He said the boat gave out a "queer hissing sound before the explosion. Then came the report, followed by a rumbling, hissing sound. Fragments of timber and metals flew in all directions. The fore part of the boat and cabin was completely carried away."

Guests at the hotel, local residents and anyone nearby with a boat began a rescue operation immediately. Rescued passengers were brought to shore and then taken aboard two steamers, the *Fountain* and the *Annie*, which came to the rescue to transport the survivors and the victims to Mobile. The two boats had been met by Captain John Payne of the sloop *Ida*, who told them of the disaster he had witnessed from a distance of about four miles. The *Ida* continued on to Mobile, where the disastrous news was reported. Some of the wounded were sent to Mobile immediately, while some were tended by many caring people at the hotel and nearby homes. Mr. and Mrs. Semple of the hotel were especially named as those who spent countless hours assisting in the rescue operation and caring for the wounded. Newspaper reports in Mobile described the crowds at the docks in the port city as a mob scene. Families and friends were desperately seeking news of their loved ones, and the police had to use force to keep the crowd from charging on to the vessels carrying victims.

It is still impossible to do more than estimate the number of fatalities. Data was difficult to compile in those days before passenger manifests were common. Most accounts say that there were from fifty to seventy deaths and many more injuries. As night fell, the scene remained a rescue operation, as some passengers still made their way to shore or were rescued by local boaters. Captain William Eaton swam for some time with two broken legs and went down just before a boat was able to get to him. The two pilots and all of the firemen were killed. The engineer and his wife were severely injured. Of the Creole family of Gaston Nicholas, six of the seven family members onboard were killed. The catastrophe was one that no witness could ever forget. The mutilated and burned bodies made for nightmares for survivors and rescuers as well. The remnants of the boat and its human cargo were found for a long time afterward. One of the saddest aspects is the report of an eyewitness who described the shoreline, where little hats and baby bonnets washed ashore. Shoes, bags and items of clothing were found all along the beach for several weeks.

The phantom explosion is rarely seen by paranormal groups or those who know about the history of the tragedy. It seems that most sightings are by those innocent and unexpecting guests at the hotel who are gathering at sunset on the shoreline—those on an excursion, perhaps. They see a glow at a short distance out in the bay, just when the sun is setting. Most assume that it is the sunlight playing on the bay waters in brilliant reds and oranges. Some witness the intense displays and ask about the fireworks out in the bay.

For more information on the bay boat era, see She's Bound to be a Goer *by Peco Forsman, published by Creekhouse Publishing, PO Box 191, Silverhill, Alabama, in 2014. ISBN 978-0-9913273-2-4.*

PART IV
SOUTHERN BALDWIN COUNTY

The lands south of Point Clear were first settled by watermen, hunters and trappers. Bon Secour (or Safe Harbor) was named by the earliest French to make their homes there, and Weeks Bay was a retreat for the wealthy French families of Mobile. The mouth of Mobile Bay became the location of a strategically placed fort, and residents on the shores of the Gulf of Mexico lived off the bounty of the saltwater gulf. Soon the warm climate, beautiful waterways and opportunities for growth led to the development of resorts along the rivers, such as the Magnolia River, where many Chicagoans came to escape the Windy City for a summer getaway. Fishing was the main source of income for the residents until forestry industries began to grow, with naval stores and lumber businesses sprouting up. The people who lived here were people of the water and forests. The heritage of these people was preserved by oral tradition, mostly on the front porches of dogtrot cabins. Let me tell you about this heritage.

THE CREOLE ROSARY: WEEKS BAY

Gramere Weeks was a fine lady who reared her seven Creole children in her little cabin on Weeks Bay. She and her husband lived in the community where most of the residents were descendants of the earliest French settlers in Alabama. Some Creoles had land grants in the southern part of the county, and others lived in Mobile and came to Weeks Bay for respite and retreat. Jolina lived her simple life performing the duties of a loving mother and wife with a regal bearing, cleaning the fish and game her husband brought home and using recipes handed down from her family—lots of spices and peppers in every dish. There were rumors that Jolina was of royal blood, having fled France during the revolution. If so, she adapted well to the New World and her new life.

The children learned survival skills that enabled them to live in the wild country, living off the land and sea, even though Gaston managed a successful shipping business, having offices in Mobile and New Orleans. Religion was so important to Jolina that she carried her rosary in her apron pocket at all times. She attended Mass regularly at her parish church, St. John's Roman Catholic Church, where the children also attended the parish school. Even with the sophistication of their heritage, their home remained a humble refuge typical of the Creole homes in the area. They did not put on airs or flout their good fortunes. They lived simple lives where the family always came first in any decision.

Jolina lived a long, productive, beautiful life for more than eighty-five years. As she grew older and more feeble, she could often be seen fingering the beads and muttering the Latin prayers that guided her life. Each night, she placed the rosary in a cupboard case built in the headboard of their bed. She passed on a Sunday, a peaceful departure, with many of her children and her beloved Gaston around her. She died holding that ruby red rosary. In the days that followed, after her body was embalmed and returned to the cabin, the family began their custom of holding a prayer vigil several evenings before the funeral. Relatives from near and far came to sit in the house and pray the rosary at 5:00 p.m. and then stay for dinner.

On Friday evening after dinner, Gaston stood by the coffin with two of his daughters. He remembered that Jolina wanted to be buried with her precious rosary and went to retrieve it from the bookcase headboard. However, it was not there. Alarmed, he asked all the family members to help in the search for the red beads, and for at least an hour, more than thirty people searched the small house from top to bottom. Distraught at having lost the most precious of all her possessions, Gaston was not able to stop the tears rolling down his ruddy cheeks into his full white beard. His children persuaded him to try to get some sleep, so he lay down on his side of the bed that the couple had shared for more than sixty years. As the morning light began to creep into the bedroom, Gaston awoke with a broken heart once again and lay there staring at the ceiling and praying for Jolina. He looked at Jolina's side of the bed, but her empty pillow brought him only sorrow.

The funeral was a celebration of the legacy that Jolina had created, and the community joined in the prayers and hymns. The reception held afterward at the house hosted more than two hundred visitors who feasted on gumbo and cornbread cakes. As the guests left and the house once again became quiet, Gaston went to bed and wept until he finally fell asleep. As he awoke the next morning, a Sunday, he naturally turned his head to look at the pillow that once cradled his precious Jolina's head. He sat up right away, for a wonderful present was there on the pillow for him. His eyes rested on her ruby red rosary. He felt a peace flow over his heart as he reached to touch the holy beads. They felt warm, and he knew that Jolina would always be alive to him. Wanting to fulfill her wishes, he took the rosary to the cemetery that very morning. He buried it in the freshly dug dirt so that it would be close to her. He knew that she would know it was there. He told only a few people of this miracle.

Gaston lived some years longer, walking every day to the cemetery to talk to Jolina and mutter a quiet prayer. Soon he was able to have a slab placed over her grave—a plain cement rectangle, unpretentious, just as she had lived her life. Gradually, he began to notice that spots of a red coloration were starting to appear on the slab. They were somewhat round and were near one another. Day after day, he scrubbed the red spots away, only to have them return within a short period of time. He asked his daughter to help him clean the grave marker, but she had little success as well. Now Gaston and Jolina lie side by side in the cemetery under matching unmarked concrete slabs. Their daughter continued to clean the slab after her father's death, but the spots always returned. You can find the graves if you find a pair of concrete slabs in the Creole cemetery, one looking as if a part of it has been scrubbed so much that the concrete is hollowed out. The stones revealed in the concrete almost look red. Even if some descendant cleans the graves on Decoration Day, the ruby red rosary spots always return.

OL' TWO TOE: DELTA BAYOUS

Many Creole watermen in Bon Secour know well the story of Ol' Two Toe. Alligator lore has long been the subject of many stories about life in the bayous, swamps and deltas of the South, but the true story of Two Toe tops them all. Two Toe was so famous that many other locales claimed him as their own, but Baldwin County locals know the truth. Two Toe was a monster 'gator first talked about in the early 1900s, when fishermen began to witness huge alligator slides, marks made by the animal as it moves in and out of the water. As shrimpers and oystermen set out during the night, they often saw giant red eyes on the banks of the Bon Secour River.

The Creole people who lived along the Bon Secour were descendants of the earliest French explorers to come to Alabama. The rivers and bay were teeming with fish, oysters and shrimp that almost jumped into the boats, and the swamplands held animals whose furs were in high demand across the ocean. Riverside residents there regularly set traps for beavers, raccoons or bears for their fur trade. One morning, a strange sight awaited the Bertrand boys as they checked their traps: a part of the foot of an alligator was in the trap. Evidently, a large 'gator caught his right rear foot in the trap and pulled himself free, leaving two of his toes behind. The Bertrands nailed the two toes to the side of their barn for all to see for years to come.

Soon, people began noticing tracks in some of the alligator slides that indicated a twelve-foot alligator with only two toes on one of his hind legs. It was not long before people began to see a large, aggressive alligator on land actually chasing small animals. Anyone who knows alligators knows that they just do not do that sort of thing, so alarming tales began to spread about the amazing characteristics of this reptile. One farmer trying to save his pig from the 'gator swore that he was close enough to see the alligator's back right foot, which had only its two outside toes; the two middle toes were missing. He failed to save his pig, as the 'gator ran so fast he disappeared into the swamp.

Word spread like wildfire to waterfront dwellers—"Be on the lookout for Ol' Two Toe. He will steal your animals and chase your children. Shoot him on sight." Of course, all missing animals and even missing children were attributed to the exploits of Two Toe. Sightings of him continued, as he seemed to move north up Weeks Bay and Fish River, across Minette Bay and on up into the Tensaw River Delta area. Residents in the northern part of the county began to swear that an alligator could be seen running so fast across their land that he could lift up his front legs and run on his hind legs just like a human being. Some auto travelers even related that they would look out the car windows late at night and see an alligator running on its back legs, keeping up with the speed of the car.

For a while, there were stories of the killing of Two Toe. A 1930 article in the *Onlooker* gave a description of a successful alligator hunt:

> *ALLIGATORS ARE CAUGHT IN BALDWIN TOO*
>
> *This 13 foot alligator weighing between 800 and 1000 pounds, was caught Saturday afternoon, September 6 at the mouth of Boggy Branch and Bon Secour River by Van and Quitman Cooper. Van said Harry Weeks had shot at the monster earlier in the day, but missed him. About 4 o'clock that afternoon the Cooper brothers went down to the river hunting him, spied him and cut loose with a shotgun. After being shot, the gator submerged and didn't come up for thirty minutes. When he came up, he was about five yards away and Van shot him again. After he went down the second time, Quitman went under and tied a rope around him. Then, with the help of two outboard motors, he was pulled across the river and pulled partly out of the water. About an hour later, after having him tied to the beach, the huge fellow came to life again and tried to get away. He was shot a third time, which quieted him for good.*
>
> *It took seven men to load the alligator, Cooper said, and an estimate by one person said he must be well over two hundred years old.*
>
> *Cooper said he heard that M.B. Jones was almost overturned in his boat about a week previous when the alligator, or one of his clan, came under the middle of the boat from which he was fishing and gave it a tremendous knock.*
>
> *The carcass was given to the state to be mounted and put on display at the state museum at Montgomery.*

The Cooper brothers were certainly hoping that this monster alligator was missing two toes on his rear foot, but this 'gator was totally intact.

The members of the Weeks family were some of the most productive alligator hunters in the county. The hides brought in a fair income during the first half of the twentieth century. Now, the story goes that one of those Weeks boys caught an alligator of unusual length. He bragged to everyone that he had killed Ol' Two Toe. In fact, he cut off the right rear foot of the alligator, put it in a gallon pickle jar of alcohol (probably of moonshine liquor quality) and put it on display in Patterson's store at Swift Landing. People shopping at the store were dismayed at the size of the foot stuffed into the glass jar. Unfortunately, or perhaps fortunately, one day the jar was knocked to the floor and shattered. Norvell Patterson picked up the foot for

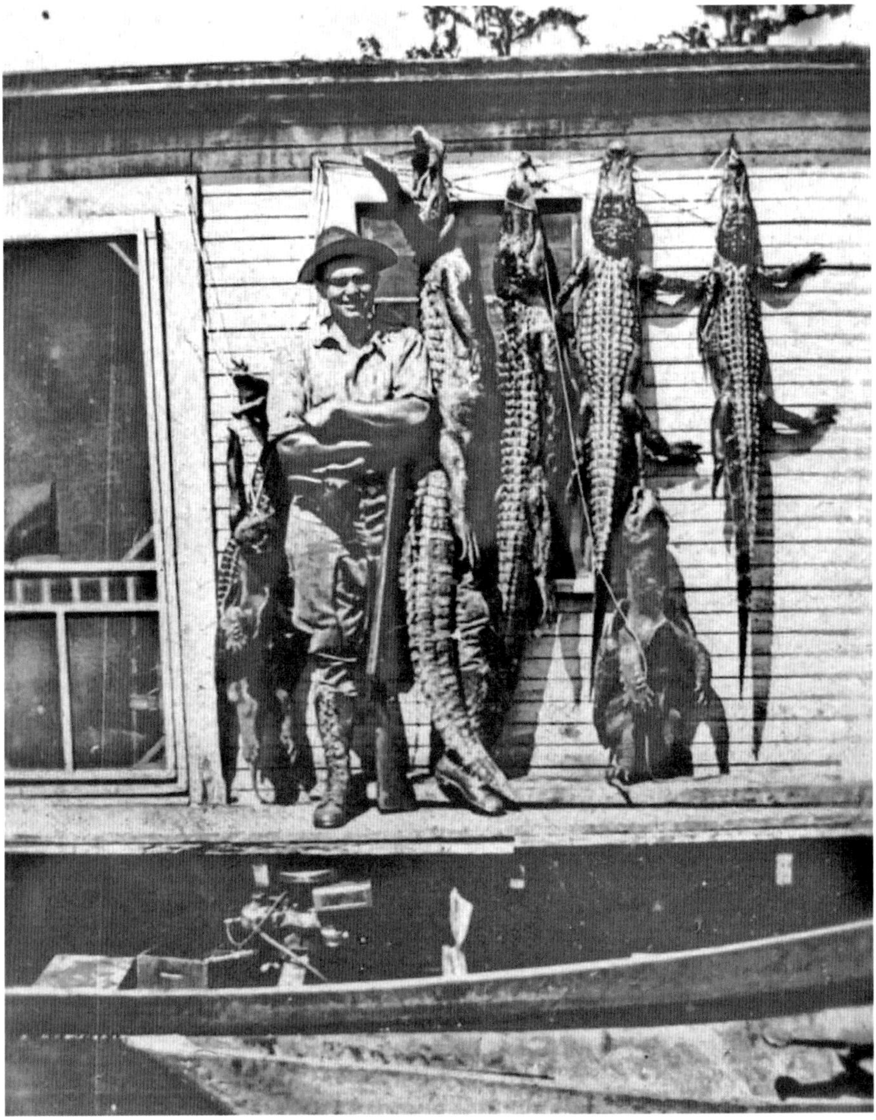

Alligator hunter displays his 'gator hides drying. *Author's collection.*

a really close look and discovered that the foot had been "doctored" with stitches across the place where the missing toes had been. So the story that Ol' Two Toe was dead was dispelled, and the legend continued to grow.

So Ol' Two Toe was indeed still alive and wreaking havoc wherever he chose. Tales of Two Toe stealing mules and calves ran rampant throughout

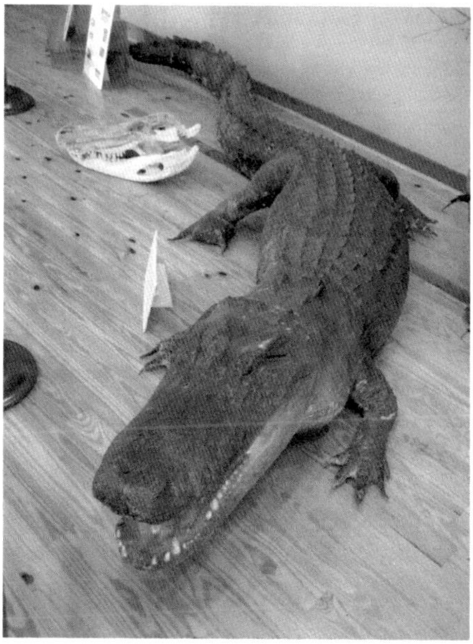

Ol' Two Toe—or one of his offspring—is on display at Five Rivers Delta Center, Highway 98, Spanish Fort. *Photo by Penny H. Taylor.*

the twentieth and into the twenty-first centuries. Hunters in the delta area told of finding partly eaten deer alongside alligator nests in the swamps. People even feared for the lives of their children. In fact, sightings of smaller 'gators with only two right rear toes began to surface. The old folks said that Ol' Two Toe's babies were born with only two toes.

Even when alligators were declared endangered and hunting was prohibited, all Baldwin County outdoorsmen knew that they would risk jail if they could just rid the area of this horrible nuisance. In 2006, alligator hunting was made legal with very specific regulations. The first year's season brought fame to a group of men who nailed a record alligator. The 461-pound, twelve-foot, four-inch alligator was killed by David Lenor, Butch Samson and Ronald Davenport in the Bay Minette Basin. That alligator was put on display at the Five Rivers Delta Center on the causeway on Mobile Bay.

And that is where he is seen today. Go see his right rear foot for yourself; see the two toes that are remaining. Ask where the other two toes are. You may get an answer, or you may choose to believe that which is true. Is this really Two Toe, or maybe one of his descendants? Did the "two toe mutation" carry on to his next generation? The specter of Two Toe is still seen often along the swamps of the Tensaw River. When a hunter gets close enough to be assured that the right hind foot has only two toes, the monster rises up on his hind feet and evaporates into the misty swamp. Fishermen in the delta know that if they see two red eyes farther apart than they think possible, they need make haste back home, for the sighting bears omen of death to come. If the evil eyes make contact with the fishermen, they are sure to face drowning and become the alligator's next meal.

THE LADY ON THE STAIRS: SWIFT-COLES HOUSE

Where Schoolhouse Creek flows into the Bon Secour River, there stands a grand home: the Swift-Coles House. The rambling house was once full of the sounds of the eleven children of Charles and Susan Swift. Charles and Susan were married in Mobile in 1885 and lived in several places before settling down in the southern part of Baldwin County near one of the Swift Lumber Company sawmills. Charles and Susan moved their family into a dogtrot cabin that was near the mill. The Swifts added on to the cabin, even adding a second story to accommodate their large family. One can imagine what life was like there in the early part of the twentieth century: doors open to the expansive porches, delicious smells coming from the kitchen and lots of laughter inside and out. When riverboats stopped at the landing, Mrs. Swift often greeted the passengers and invited them to come up to the house. Mrs. Swift was certainly a busy lady with gracious charm in her lovely home.

Susan was a loving mother who encouraged her children to be the best they could be, and they did indeed carry on the family code of excellence. Several of the children lived in the house after they were grown and married,

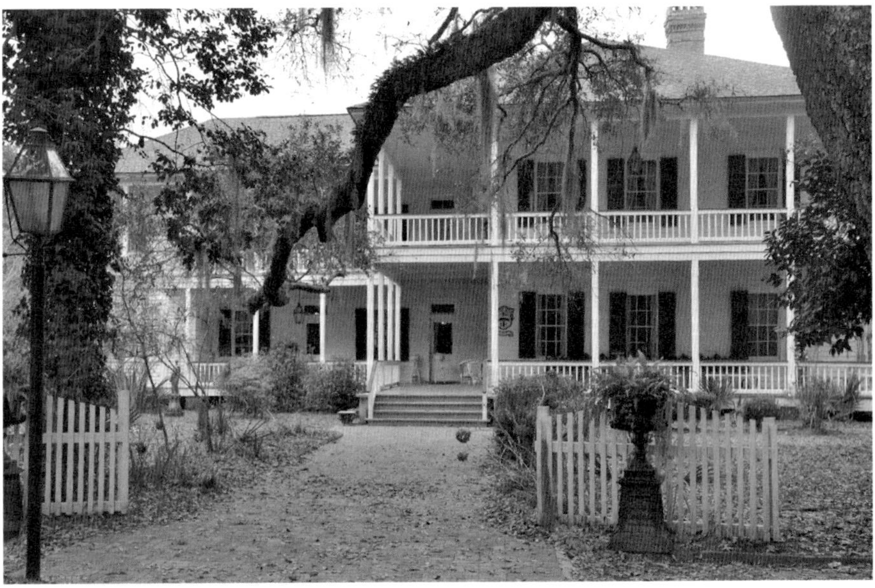

The Swift-Coles House was donated to the Baldwin County Historic Development Commission by Nik Coles. *Photo by Penny H. Taylor.*

and grandchildren and cousins came for extended visits to the homeplace on the banks of the river. During World War II, three families of Swifts lived in the home. Meme (Swift) and Charles Wakeford were known to host local servicemen for seafood dinners, and later they opened the famous Meme's Restaurant on the banks of the Bon Secour. William and Ione were living in the home when their daughter Ione was born in 1939, and Emily cared for little Ione while the parents worked. By 1949, Susie Nell Swift Marshall and her husband were living there and continuing to maintain the family home as the hub of a large extended family. Throughout all these years, the front parlor was kept as the formal sitting room, and the family desk remained in that room the entire time.

In 1976, after Susie Nell died, the house was purchased by Mr. Nik Coles, who immediately began a refurbishment of the home. He had always admired the home and was passionate about its preservation. He told others that he used to come park in the driveway and dream of life in that house. He even had plans to build a replica of the house before it came on the market. Mr. Coles never married but often laughed that he had a lifetime affair with the Big House.

One of the first tasks he undertook was to strip the interior walls of the house of the many layers of paint that had been applied for almost one hundred years. The Swift family heirs were in the process of moving the precious family heirlooms and furniture even after Nik had begun the restoration process. Nik hired workmen who began with the removal of the bookcases in the central hall of the oldest part of the house, the room known as the library. They were busy with their work—electric saws buzzing, crowbars creaking and hammers knocking away at the wood. As they worked on a hot July afternoon, they were astounded when there suddenly arose a lightning storm that sent a cold wind through the hallway. The lights flickered and then went out. Their power tools were silenced, and the men felt frozen in the cold, dark room. A light at the top of the stairs caught their eye, and as each turned his face up, he saw that the light was coming from the lovely white hair of an elegant lady who began to descend the staircase. In the quiet of the afternoon, she walked slowly and gracefully down the stairs. They could hear her dress rustle as she stepped on each stair tread. She wore a high-necked white blouse and a long black skirt. Her hair was held away from her face with combs and was secured in a knot on top of her head. As she reached the landing, she looked at the men, who had ceased their work and stood staring at this woman wearing clothing many years out of fashion. As her blue eyes looked directly at the workmen, they each sensed that she was questioning what they were doing there. At that moment, the men said that they heard her ask, "Gentlemen, what are you doing to my library?"

As she approached the men, they backed up from her, and as she passed by them, headed toward the front parlor, they felt frozen in place by a cloud of cold air surrounding them. She was gradually becoming more and more indistinguishable, and as the lady reached the closed door of the parlor, she seemed to melt through the wood of the door. The gentlemen quickly left their tools and departed immediately, never to return.

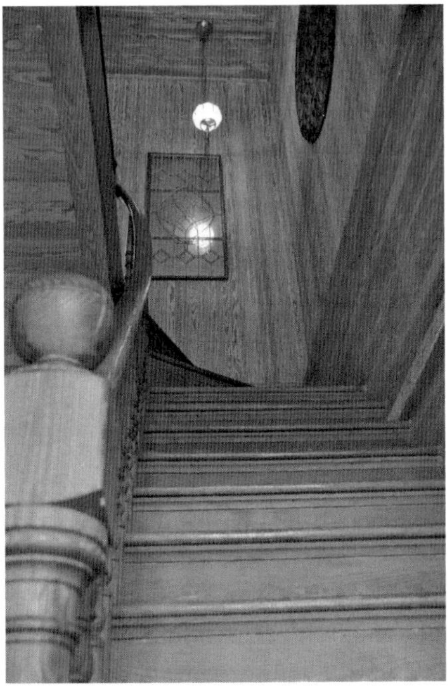

It has been said that a lady has been seen descending the stairway in the Swift-Coles Historic Home. *Photo by Penny H. Taylor.*

Within a few days of the lady's appearance to the workmen, one of the Swift heirs from Atmore came to pick up an heirloom bequeathed to him: the parlor desk. Upon his arrival, Mr. Coles told him of the strange event with the workmen. Mr. Swift did not believe the story told by Mr. Coles, who was known as a good storyteller, and began to load the precious piece of furniture onto the bed of the truck that he had backed up to the east door. While carrying the desk to the truck, the mover suddenly fell, suffering a sprained ankle. As the task progressed, more mishaps occurred. The truck had a flat tire, and the top of the desk was blown off the truck. As the movers worked to get the desk into the home in Atmore, it had to be disassembled to fit through the door. Finally, the desk was placed in its new home in the guest bedroom. The new owner reported that, looking back, he had noticed unusual occurrences in the bedroom, such as the sound of pages turning. Sometimes he would hear a door open and close, but he thought very little of it until he finally realized there was a presence living there. One morning at breakfast, his daughter's fiancé asked the identity of the woman staying in the guest bedroom. He had seen her the previous night at the end of the hall entering the bedroom. He had followed her and saw her sitting at the family desk.

The desk must have a powerful meaning to the beautiful lady with white hair who continues to care for her family's business at the heirloom desk. Who is she? One can only speculate. Even though the desk is no longer present in the Swift family home, the loving feelings of a happy family persist there—perhaps other spirits. After the home was opened as a museum in 2009, docents have heard stories from guests who had been to the house in earlier years. Some people say that they have seen the figure of Mary, a devoted lady who helped care for the children and cook. She was seen smoothing coverlets over beds, as if tucking a child in for the night. Some workmen reported that doors closed as they approach them and became locked. One docent recently had an uncanny experience in the upstairs master bedroom. Scissors on a piece of furniture flew off the stand and hit the floor spinning—that has happened three times to this docent. Others have since reported the scissors being found on the floor. The loveliest stories of all are from those who hear children playing in the yard. The squeals of laughter and voices that seem to say, "Tag, you're it," help all who hear them remember that the sounds of happiness live forever.

The Swift-Coles Historic Home is open to the public for tours. It is located at the southern end of County Road 49 on the Bon Secour River. See www.swiftcoleshistorichome.com.

THE LADY IN A BLUE DRESS: FORT MORGAN

Way down at the southwestern tip of the county, at the end of a peninsula, stands the most haunted fort in America, according to many experts on the subject. There have certainly been more reports written about sightings at Fort Morgan than at any other spot in Baldwin County. The dark and eerie passageways lend themselves to active imaginations, but people swear that the apparitions they saw or the sounds they heard were very real. Ghost hunters, visitors and fort staff members witness strange things, most of which have known roots in the history of the fort.

The fort is a Third System Coastal Defense Fort, built on the site where earlier defense structures had been located at the strategic mouth of Mobile Bay. During the War of 1812, the United States constructed a sand and wooden fort there named for Colonel Bowyer. The British captured Fort Bowyer in 1815 after losing the Battle of New Orleans. It was returned to

U.S. possession with the peace treaty after the war. The War of 1812 made the United States realize the necessity of coastline defense, and plans were made to build the star-shaped fort, which was not completed until 1837. It saw little action until the War Between the States, when it became a most valuable installation. It guarded the entrance to Mobile Bay, along with its sister, Fort Gaines, across the channel on Dauphin Island. A famous naval battle took place there in August 1864. Admiral Farragut led his ships into the channel, where the ironclad *Tecumseh* hit a mine and sank. This was when the famous line, "Damn the torpedoes, full speed ahead," was reportedly commanded by Farragut. The Union claimed a victory, and by August 9, the Union troops had landed east of the fort and had begun the attack from land. Confederates resisted until August 23.

After the war, the fort was placed in caretaker status. It was activated during the Spanish-American War, World War I and World War II and then was deeded to the State of Alabama in 1946. The majority of spectral appearances have been related to soldiers. Figures are seen, felt and heard throughout the fort, and more than one visitor has heard a man crying in the barracks, where a man hanged himself. Some have heard scratching and moans of wounded soldiers, and quite a few have seen shadowy figures.

One of the more colorful characters in Baldwin County history is buried on the grounds of Fort Morgan. Hatchett Chandler was curator, historian and proponent of the fort in its earliest days of public access. He served more than twenty-five years and promoted the fort through his writings, *Little Gems from Fort Morgan*. He became known as a somewhat controversial figure, as his writings often disputed opinions of other historians. One such conjecture was his firm belief that Prince Madoc of Wales was the first to discover America and founded a colony at Gulf Shores. Many followers of this theory are very much active in pursuing the search for valid proof that the colony did exist and became a part of the Mandan Indian tribes.

Another of his *Little Gems* is titled "The Lost Cemetery," and this one is not the subject of controversy. Chandler wrote of a Mr. Matt Stark of Madison, Wisconsin, who paid a visit to the fort soon after World War II. He told Chandler that he had landed there in 1898 during the Spanish-American War, in which he served with the Battery 1, First U.S. Artillery, stationed at Fort Morgan. He walked the fort with Chandler and particularly described the construction of Battery Bowyer, which he helped build about one-fourth of a mile east of the old fort. He said that in excavating dirt to be thrown up against the new fort, countless human bones were uncovered. They were stacked up on the walls of the fort and were eventually reburied.

Stark could not pinpoint the location of the new burial ground. Many times, spirits are seen walking the parapets of the battery built in 1898. Chandler expressed a desire that the state erect a monument to those lost bodies, but that has never been completed.

Hatchett Chandler had obtained permission to be buried at the site of the Lost Cemetery, but after his death in 1967, his friends thought it more meaningful to have him buried much closer to the old brick fort, near a historic monument that had been erected there. The controversy that Chandler seemed to instigate did not die with him, as the burial was disputed. The funeral was scheduled for Sunday, but the procession was met with a resolution from the State Historical Commission forbidding the burial so near the fort. So, after a sermon and eulogy, the body was returned to the mortuary in Foley. Two days later, a second funeral was held without incident at the spot chosen by Chandler's friends one hundred feet east of the main wall. Surely Hatchett is still seen at the fort.

Another story, one that is not related to military conflict, is told by one of the former staff employees. He has seen a lady in a blue dress walking, or rather floating, across the parade ground. Others have seen her up on the walls of the fort—always on a cold night with a full moon. A gentleman

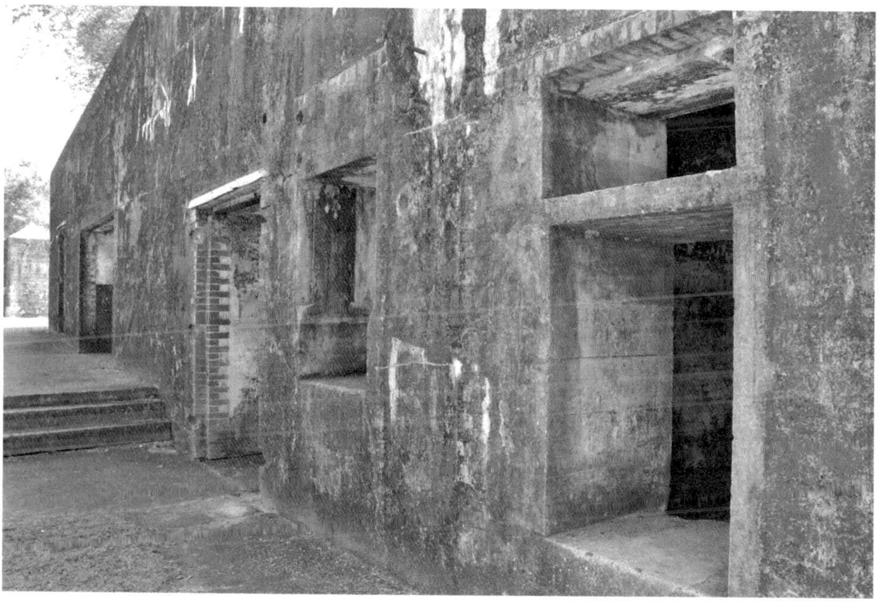

Eerie passageways at Fort Morgan are the locations of hundreds of ghostly experiences. The fort is at the western end of the Fort Morgan Peninsula, Gulf Shores. *Photo by Penny H. Taylor.*

named Louis Pepin came to visit the fort in his latter years. He wanted to see once again the place where he was born while his father was stationed there when the fort was training young men in 1914. Louis's father was sent to Hawaii for duty during World War I and returned to Fort Morgan as commanding officer when Louis was about eight. Louis and his brother witnessed the discovery of the body of a young woman on the beach. She was dressed in a flowing blue gown. The commanding officers had no luck in finding out the identity of the girl, and her body was buried in the northwest corner of the fort. Since that time, she has reappeared on many a cold, dark night. There have also been stories of the vision of a girl in a long blue flowing dress running along the beach, screaming and appearing to be trying to escape pursuers. Perhaps some of the many who come to search for ghosts at the fort will be able to find out who she is and help her—on a cold night when the moon is full.

Historic Fort Morgan, Guardian on the Bay, is an amazing place. For more information, the website is available at www.fortmorgan.org. The History Press publication Haunted Alabama Battlefields *by Langella contains stories of military sightings.*

CATMAN TRAIL: GULF SHORES STATE PARK

Campers at Gulf Shores State Park often sit around the campfires and tell stories about sightings of the Catman, but few have really seen him, at least lately.

Long before there were campsites at Gulf Shores, and even before there was a state park there, a few brave settlers chose to make their homes on the peninsula. One of these was Billy Morgan, who brought his new wife to the warm climate all the way from Pennville, Indiana. Billy had finally saved enough money to buy a little place of his own and saw an advertisement in the local paper for cheap farmsteads way down near the Gulf of Mexico. Land developers had purchased large tracts of land all along the new spur railroad line that ran right down the center of the county, opening up acreage for new settlers. Advertisements throughout the Midwest promised a piece of paradise.

The price looked right, and the magnetism of the ocean worked its magic on Bill and Nancy. They loaded their few possessions and boarded a train headed south in 1910. They took the L&N Homeseekers Excursion out of Bay Minette, a free passage to meet real estate agents in towns all the way down to the end of the line in Foley. The two were determined to go as far south as they could, so they told their agent that they wanted to see the Gulf of Mexico. It was love at first sight, and Billy and Nancy Mae purchased land on Lake Shelby. As one of the very few residents in the area, they had little contact with the outside world, but they were so very happy in the cabin they had built with their own hands. Billy and Nancy were subsistence farmers and fishermen, living off the land and sea. The couple was thrilled when a baby boy was born; Billy made him a large cradle in the shape of a boat, and Nancy Mae often sang him to sleep while rocking the cradle. They took such joy in watching their little boy learn to walk and even swim and were especially watchful of him near the woods. He seemed to have a fascination with the seaside forest growth and would sometimes slip away from his parents to explore. Occasionally, they would take their boat down to Orange Beach to pick up a few supplies and gather their mail from the post office. In the fall of 1916, however, they had not seen a soul in a week. Being newcomers to the coast in those days before telephone and electricity in Gulf Shores, they just did not know how to watch for signs of impending storms. The great hurricane hit the coast and swept their cabin out to sea; Billy and Nancy Mae were never seen again. All assumed that the baby perished with his parents, but eventually stories began to circulate about sightings of a strange creature in the woods.

People say that the cradle boat had carried the boy safely into the woods, where it lodged in the fork of a live oak tree as the boy slept through the storm. They say that he was adopted by a mother panther. You know that wild animals do very unusual things just before and after hurricanes. She must have taught him to hunt, to survive in the sandy wilderness and, especially, to be wary of human beings. Evidently, she did her job well because ten years later, during the 1926 hurricane, the rescue crew reported a young man up in a tree. When they approached him to take him to safety, he fled from them deep into the swampy forest. They said that he had long, dark hair and ran on two feet, but also on all fours as well. They were amazed at the speed at which he climbed and ran.

By the 1930s, automobiles were rapidly becoming the transportation of choice, and roadways were likewise improved. The first real road from Gulf Shores to Orange Beach was completed during the 1930s, and vacationers and locals alike became common in the area. The intracoastal canal was completed in 1937, and a cantilevered bridge was built to connect the Gulf Shores area with the rest of the state. Alabama purchased more than one thousand acres between Highway 59 and State Highway 161 to establish the Gulf State Park. The park included beachfront property on the Gulf of Mexico and also three spring-fed freshwater lakes, including Lake Shelby. Primitive roads followed the trails already established by Native Americans and animals. Local residents and tourists began to vacation at the park, and day visitors enjoyed swimming in the Gulf and the lakes.

Narratives about the longhaired and bearded man continued to be told around the stores and churches where people would gather. He was seen most often along the road running east–west in the park. It was said that if the creature were caught in the headlights of a car, he disappeared with unbelievable speed into the dark roadside woods. It was said that this creature, both man and beast, had extraordinary powers of running and especially climbing trees like a panther—thus he was soon known as Catman. The road has been named Catman Road. The county road was officially closed in the 1970s but was still a primitive roadbed until it was converted to a biking and hiking trail in 2008.

During World War II, local Gulf Telephone Operators were trained as militia forces and guarded the Gulf Coast in case of foreign military invasion. Several of them said that during the night, they would sense a presence behind them, and as they turned, they would see a shadowy figure mystically disappear back into the woods. They reported that his hair and beard were exceptionally long and seemed to cover his entire body.

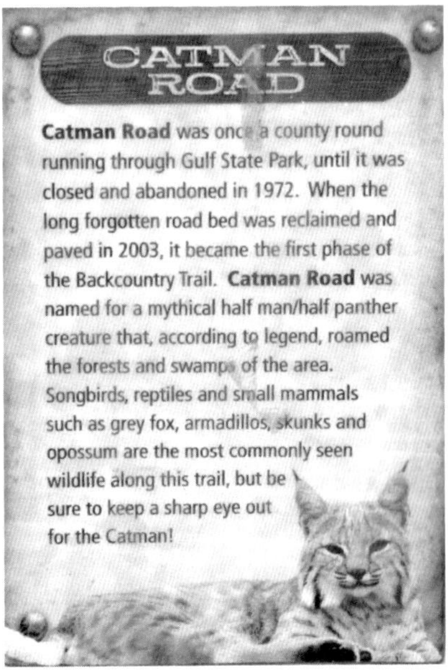

Sign posted at the entrance to Catman Trail, Gulf Shores State Park. *Photo by Penny H. Taylor.*

Teenagers in the 1950s and 1960s often told stories of the Catman, and many took up the dare to drive down Catman Road around midnight. Tales flourished of couples parked on dark roads being frightened by a creature peering in through their windows. Those even more daring struck out on foot on the road or attempted to spend the night there. The spine-tingling, and possibly imaginative, episodes related the next day never claimed that the Catman had in any way harmed anyone.

What did he do? He simply looked from a distance. There are a few believable reports that he came very close to a group of campers that had a portable radio playing soft and soothing music, but when one saw him and screamed, he disappeared. The most meaningful report of all is from a mother who was camping with her family. She was sitting by the campfire late at night holding her restless baby. She was sitting in a webbed lawn rocking chair and began singing a lullaby to soothe him. When she saw the creature creeping slowly out of the woods, she assumed it was another camper and continued singing.

She warily watched him as he looked at her with old, sad eyes. She continued singing. She watched him as he sat down on his haunches, and she continued singing. She saw a tear roll down his face, and she continued singing. She watched him curl on the ground and seem to sleep. She looked at her baby in her arms, and he was asleep as well. She sat there watching over them both. Perhaps she dozed some because when she looked at the spot where Catman had slept, he was gone. He had slipped quietly back into the woods by daybreak. The mother did not tell many people about this. She felt that she had been a part of a something very special. She had learned the secret of the Catman and knew that the end of his life was probably near. She knew in her heart that he had heard his mother's lullaby once again and was at peace for at least one night in his life.

No one knows if the Catman is still alive today. It is certainly possible. Perhaps he even had children who are there in the woods of Gulf State Park—perhaps they are even part panther. Most people say that his spirit is still there searching for his parents. Park rangers often hear tales of sightings from campers. Ranger Dave will tell the story that a group of boy scouts distinctly heard the sounds of a panther fighting in the nearby woods. If you are one of those curious people who wants to find out for yourself if Catman is still there, remember that the secret is in the song:

Go to sleepy little baby
Go to sleepy little baby
When you wake,
We'll patty patty cake
And ride on the pretty little pony.

Visit www.alapark.com for visitor information for Gulf Shores State Park.

PART V

RIDING THE RAIL LINE

The train line through the northern part of the county was completed before the War Between the States but was not completed across the delta to Mobile until the 1890s. The central part of Baldwin County was scarcely populated until the L&N spur rail line was built from Bay Minette to Foley in 1905. The rail opened up towns all along its tracks and created a means for transporting produce. Thousands of people traveled from the Midwest to purchase homes and farms, and agriculture soon became the economic support of the county. Towns were developed, and at each depot, home-seekers were met with the promise of a bright future. The population of the county tripled with families moving from the north to create new lives. After a long, hard day in the fields, local people took to their porches and cooled off in rocking chairs with glasses of sweet tea. And, of course, they told their children the things that were most important to remember: the stories of their families and the stories of the strange things they had witnessed. Come sit in a rocking chair and listen to them.

RAILROAD BILL: BAY MINETTE DEPOT

The ballad of Railroad Bill has been recorded by many folksingers, such as Rambling Jack Elliott and Joan Baez, but the real story is even better than the song.

Railroad men and people living near the railroad tracks often see the shadowy figure of a tall black man walking with a limp. Sometimes he jumps on a boxcar, and sometimes he just disappears into the deep, dark pine forests. They know that this is the same Railroad Bill their grandparents had told them about—a real south Alabama outlaw who was perhaps finally killed after years of escaping the law. There are also people who say that the man was able to turn himself into all sorts of animals and that those animals are still around today—a mysterious cat that lives in a caboose or a fox that disappears when the dogs get too close.

When Oscar Brill was a little boy, his daddy took him downtown in Bay Minette to the depot to see the body of an outlaw who had been one of the most wanted men in south Alabama. His body was on display to assure people that this railroad robber's days were over.

Railroad Bill had a real name, Morris Slater, and he worked in a turpentine still for a while. Then he took up with a traveling circus, where he learned all sorts of magic tricks and was known as Bill McCoy. He really had the magic powers of conjuring, which certainly came in handy when he was running from posses in the deep piney woods. The first time he got into trouble with

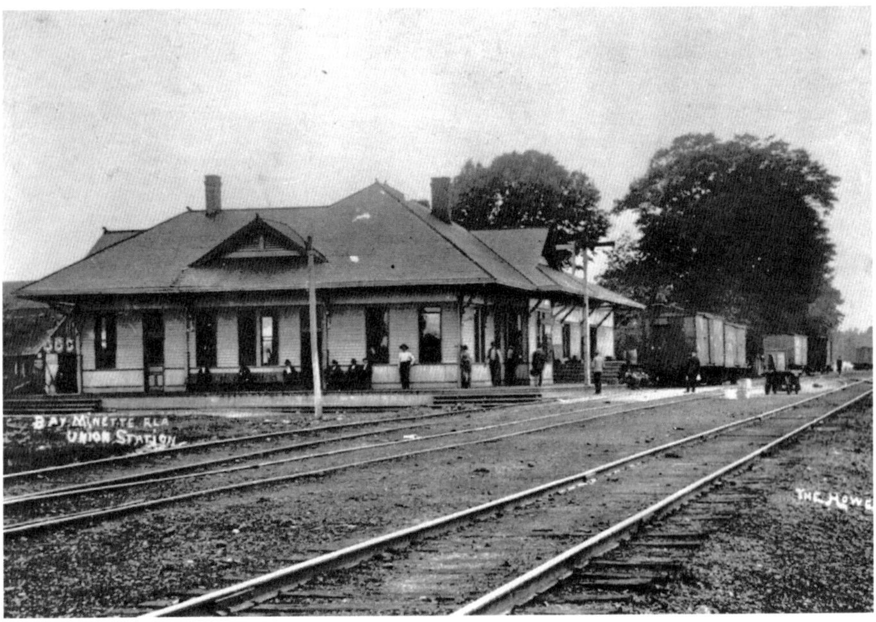

The old Bay Minette L&N Depot was located south of the courthouse. *Courtesy of John Lewis.*

the law was in the 1800s, while he was working at peckerwood sawmills and turpentine stills throughout Baldwin and Escambia Counties.

As most backwoodsmen do, Morris always carried his rifle. In fact, he carried the rifle even while he was working, stuck down his right pants leg. This made him walk with a straight-legged limp, which caught the attention of a deputy sheriff, who was determined that Morris would either purchase the required permit or relinquish the gun.

One day, the deputy came up to Morris and said, "Hand over that there rifle or else buy a permit." It is said that Morris just turned and walked away, disappearing before the deputy could grab him. Well, the deputy was then even more determined and thought that it "sure was a good-looking rifle." The next time the deputy approached him, Morris once again turned to walk away. The deputy pulled his gun and opened fire. Morris turned and fired at the deputy, shooting his ear off. Morris knew very well that he would be found guilty and sentenced to a long jail term (if he was not lynched before the trial), so he took off down the tracks. He jumped on a slow-moving freight train, and his life and name were changed forever.

He jumped off into the woods, found a hideout with some of his friends and took his old circus name, Bill McCoy. He often hitched rides on the freight trains, keeping on the move to elude the law. One time, he jumped into an open boxcar and found that it was full of cases of canned goods heading for the Hurricane Landing to cross the delta to Mobile. Knowing that he was a fugitive anyway, he picked up a few of the crates and tossed them off the train. He then jumped the train and retrieved the booty, taking it to some locals who had offered him a hideout place. The starving families were so thankful for the food that he continued this practice. In fact, he took to throwing the goods off the train so that the people living along the tracks could pick them up. These people looked forward to those gifts and began to sing the praises of this railroad outlaw, songs they sang around their fires in the evening. If Railroad Bill happened to be nearby and needed a place to hide out, he was always welcome in the homes of his people. They always had canned pork and beans to feed him that most likely had come their way via Bill's escapades.

The L&N Railroad, however, did not look at Bill in the same way. It offered a reward for Bill that eventually rose up to $1,250 and included a lifetime pass on the railroad. The Pinkerton Agency was even called in to help. An agent named Mark Stinson, a black detective, was assigned to befriend Bill and earn his trust. For a while, reports came in from Mark, but then they abruptly stopped and the agent was never heard from again.

Every sheriff who was elected had campaigned on the promise to bring down this renegade thief. Reports of murders of several pursuers were rampant, but it was difficult to prove whether they were true or propaganda against the man who was fast becoming a folk hero among the black residents of south Alabama. Banjos were brought out on the porches of the dogtrot cabins, and verses were added with each story about Bill's adventures that came their way—true or not:

Railroad Bill, Railroad Bill,
He never worked and he never will.
Railroad Bill was a mighty bad man,
Shot the light out of the brakeman's hand.

They lookin' for that bad Railroad Bill.
Oh, ride, ride, ride.

Tales of the magic powers that Bill possessed were encouraged and enhanced by Bill himself. It was said that he could turn himself into any animal he chose and that only a silver bullet would claim his life. One sheriff in Escambia County, Ed McMillan, declared that he would take the notorious thief and murderer, dead or alive. Later, Sheriff McMillan got a strange note: "I wish you hadn't made that statement, Mr. Ed, because I love you and don't want to kill you, so don't come after me." Bill did shoot Ed McMillan when he came after him, and it was reported in the *Standard Gauge* on July 4, 1895:

At twelve o'clock last night, E.S. McMillan died from effects of a shot fired by the notorious outlaw, Railroad Bill. Sheriff McMillan had been endeavoring to capture "Railroad," who has been beating about Bluff Springs, Bay Minette and Flomaton. Parties were keeping him supplied with ammunition and knowledge of the movement of the officers. Sheriff McMillan knew it would be a difficult capture but, hearing that "Railroad" was in Molino, he, Dr. O. Brannon and son, Charles, went down to hunt him. They located him near Bluff Springs. When they started to the house, someone called "Who's there?" and then fired, hitting no one. Sheriff McMillan came from behind a tree and raised his gun, when another shot hit him through the heart. The other men fired, but Sheriff McMillan needed their attention. They asked him if he was hurt and he replied, "Yes, I'm killed." He was taken to John McDavid's

> *house and there asked the men to pray for him, as he would be dead shortly. Superintendent McKinney sent a special car with doctors and friends but it came too late. The body was brought to Brewton. Sheriff McMillan was the fifth son of Malcolm McMillan.*

Verses to the folksong were added:

> *Railroad Bill cut a might dash,*
> *Shot McMillan by a lightning flash.*
> *Ride, ride, ride.*
> *Ride on, Railroad Bill.*
>
> *Railroad Bill was a might spo't,*
> *Shot the buttons off the lawman's coat.*
> *Ride, ride, ride.*
> *Ride on, Railroad Bill.*

The search was intensified. Every time that a lawman would get close to Railroad Bill deep in the piney woods, he would somehow slip away. One time, they saw a cat run out of the house where they knew Bill was hiding, and no sign of Bill was found inside the house. Another time, when dogs were fast on his scent, a strange dog joined the pack, causing them to lose their trail. Everyone around knew that Railroad Bill could conjure himself and often did. Yes, indeed, one time he became a fox whose laugh even sounded just like Bill's, and other times he changed into a sheep or a mule and just watched as the posse rode by hot on the trail of Railroad Bill.

The hunt for Railroad Bill ended when a man was shot in Tidmore and Ward's General Store in Atmore. There are several accounts of this killing. Some say that a posse happened into the store, and one deputy recognized Bill sitting on a barrel eating cheese and crackers. Others say that Leonard McGowan and A.C. John had been tipped off to where Bill was hiding out and waited to ambush him. John fired first, and the man fell to the floor. When McGowan entered, he fired again at the prone man lying there in a pool of blood on the wooden planks of the country store, distorting his face.

The L&N agent at the Atmore Depot rushed there and took the body to the funeral home, where it was embalmed. They did not bury him right away but instead put the body on a flatbed rail car. Old folks say that Constable J.L. McGowan posed with the body strapped to a wooden plank. Souvenir hunters paid fifty cents for a copy of that photo.

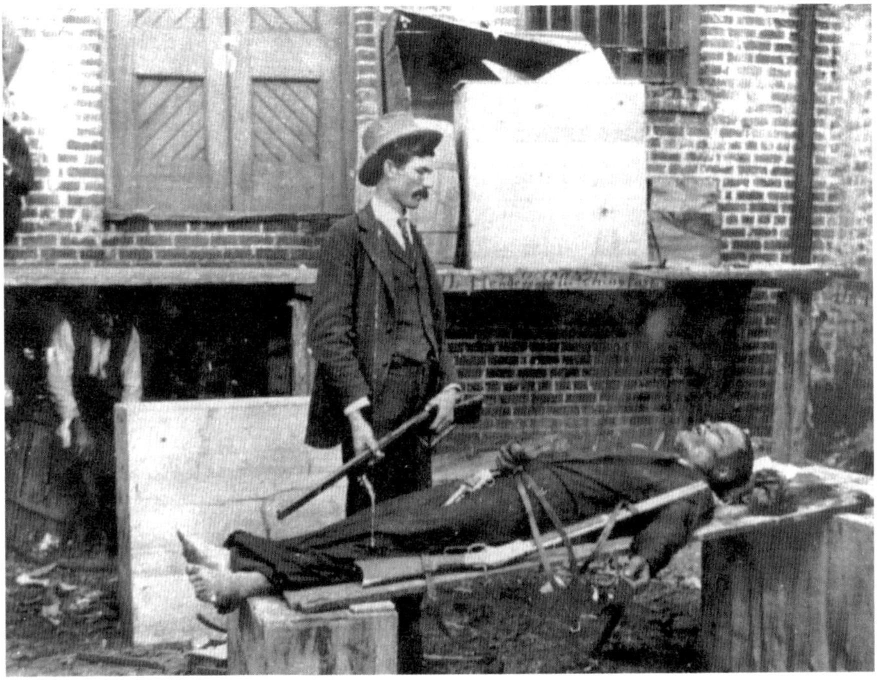

The reported body of Railroad Bill was displayed at train stops throughout Escambia and Baldwin Counties to reassure passengers that an end had come to the outlaw's train robbing days. *Author's collection.*

The death train with the flatbed car traveled all along the rail line that Bill knew well. The people in Brewton, Atmore, Flomaton and Perdido filed by to view the body and were all assured that this dangerous man was really gone. Well, some were. Many who looked at the body said that there was no way it could be Wild Bill McCoy. At the Bay Minette Depot, the last scheduled stop of the tour, Bill's coffin was placed on the loading dock of the warehouse part of the depot. While his body lay there in the coffin, Oscar noticed a gray cat under the coffin bier, just looking as smug and content as a cat can look. The cat strolled among the crowd, walked down the track a little ways, jumped up in the caboose and went to sleep. When Oscar looked back at the body in the coffin, a strange feeling came over him, and he began trembling. For in the coffin the body was covered with a layer of mist and was not visible. The men at the station immediately closed the lid of the coffin, looking at one another with questioning faces. Oscar swore that just as the lid was closing, he witnessed the vapor escape the coffin, leaving an empty pillow inside. The deputies shuttled the coffin off to a potters' field

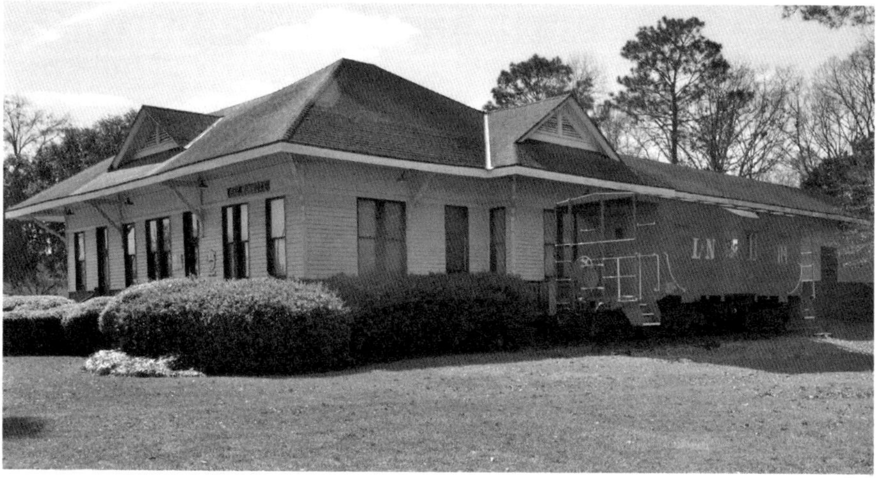

The depot in Bay Minette was salvaged and moved to Highway 59, where it serves as the office of the North Baldwin Chamber of Commerce. *Photo by Penny H. Taylor.*

and said they buried it. The grave was not marked in any way, and no one could find anyone who would admit to being there for the actual burial.

People still talk about that day—the last day that anyone saw Railroad Bill. At least, that is the last day he was seen in his human form—if that body was even really Wild Bill McCoy. If it was, it had changed into that gray tabby cat. Today at the Bay Minette Depot, which was moved from downtown out to Highway 59, you may see the gray cat that strolls around there just as cool as can be. You may see him asleep inside the caboose there, although no one knows how that cat can get into that car. The workers at the chamber of commerce there know that the cat will not let himself be touched, but they feed him nonetheless. I guess they know that all those times Railroad Bill fed the people along the tracks is worth some payback. Railroad Bill just loves that railroad depot, doesn't he?

The shadowy figure of a black man limping along the tracks is still seen by those brave enough to walk the tracks from Bay Minette to Brewton in the dead of night. Engineers have been known to lay on their whistles and apply the brakes, afraid that they are going to hit the crippled old man. But before the engine reaches him, he slips away into the woods to a dogtrot cabin to spend the night with his friends.

The original Bay Minette Depot serves as the chamber of commerce office, located on Highway 59. The red caboose is next to the depot.

THE GIRL IN THE WINDOW: LOXLEY HOTEL

Maureen, an Amish girl, was close to her family, but she would not tell them her darkest secret. She was a pure, lovely girl living on the family farm in Ohio and was a perfect child and student at the one-room school. Maureen hoped to marry a good Amish boy and live near her family. But something terrible changed her future. And she never told anyone what that was. Maureen was diligent in her chores around the farm and house. She washed walls, cleaned the stables, milked the cow, cooked the dinner and often did extra work to help her weak mother. One day, she simply disappeared.

It was not an easy step for Maureen to take. In fact, it was more than terrifying for a young girl who had never been farther than the nearby town in the family horse-drawn buggy. She wanted to protect her beloved family and felt that in giving up all she loved she would save her family the pain of disgrace her staying would bring. So, she slipped out at night, taking the money she had earned from the sale of her cheeses, and walked the three miles to the train station.

She was not completely without a plan. She had read in the community newsletter that several families had taken the train south to a place called Bay Minette, Alabama, where the land was fertile and cheap. Of course, she knew she would never be a landowner, but she hoped that there might be a place for her to find work so she could provide for the coming life she bore within her. The trip was almost unbearable. She sat in a third-class seat and munched on the dried apples she brought along when she felt the pangs of hunger meeting the fear in her belly.

A lovely lady sat next to her and began to chat. The lady asked about her but was met with nothing that would give her any hint of the girl's home or destination. The lady was a mother and had an ingrained sense that this young lady needed a friend. So, she just talked aloud about their plans to move south, saying that she and her husband had read an ad about farmland in Baldwin County. She talked about the train depot in Bay Minette, affordable hotels nearby and the free monthly Homeseekers Excursion train that they would take to see if they would settle there in the land of milk and honey.

Maureen was tired and felt dirty when the train arrived at the Bay Minette Depot, and she accompanied her new friend to the Hamilton Hotel, where she counted out the coins for the night from her meager cache and went to her room without any supper. Awake in plenty of time to be at the station for the departure of the Homeseekers Excursion, she met her new friend there on the loading platform. As the conductor called, "All aboard," the homeseekers eagerly scrambled for seats on the free ride. Of course, there was a catch to this "free ride." Homeseekers were expected to stop at one of the stations along the southbound train and meet a real estate agent, who would show them available properties in the area and promote the prospect that this was the best place to live in the world. Each town claimed that paradise was found nearby.

At the second stop on the line, Maureen could see the lovely Loxley Hotel from the passenger car. The town seemed to bustle with wagons and people, and she felt drawn to the little community, hoping to find work. With her small carpetbag holding all of her possessions, she marched with determination up the steps of the lovely building. At the desk, she spoke to the owner, deciding that the truth should be tempered with a little white lie typically used by girls in her predicament: she said that she was the widow of a soldier who lost his life in France in the recent Great War. Explaining that she had no other family, she was seeking work. Her eyes were so filled with pleading that the owner decided to give her a chance. It so happened that the hotel was in need of a housekeeper and cook at that moment, and Maureen was offered the probationary job with a small room upstairs.

Her Amish training served Maureen well. She was more than comfortable cleaning the rooms, doing the laundry and cooking the meals for the guests. Thanking God for her good fortune, she had a place to stay and food to eat. Maureen missed her family dearly but knew that if she returned, she would only be shunned and could not bear that future for her coming child. Somehow, her condition remained a secret kept under her voluminous apron until it was nearly time for her to deliver. One day, the owner of the hotel asked Maureen to come into her parlor for a little talk. Maureen went with trepidation, knowing that this would mean the end to her job and home, but she was overwhelmed when she was shown loving empathy for her situation and an offer to help. Maureen's kindness and work ethic had earned respect and admiration from the owner. Tears of appreciation rolled down her cheeks as she profusely thanked her employer.

The baby was a perfect little girl, rarely whimpering and smiling often. Maureen kept the baby in the upper room while she attended to her chores at the hotel. She went there to feed her and change her as often as she could. As the child grew, she accompanied her mother around the hotel during her work hours. Unfortunately, when the little girl was four, the understanding owner of the hotel died, and the establishment was purchased by an investor with no patience for an employee with a child in tow. He told Maureen that she could remain employed a long as the child did not interfere with her work and remained out of the way of the paying guests. So Maureen kept the child confined to the upstairs room. As the child grew, she had no contact with life outside her room. She knew of no love other than her mother's, but that was more than enough to bring the child happiness.

The child constantly held the doll her mother had made for her to keep her company while she was waiting for her mother. The little girl and her mother played a game of hiding from the outside world, but she still loved to peer out of the front window, watching the teeming bustle of life on the streets and the train come and go. Maureen consistently brought books to the little girl and taught her to read, and she read voraciously. When she began to question her mother about their confinement, Maureen knew that the time would soon come when she must change her situation in life to provide a healthy environment for her child.

Maureen began a search for another job. Every day during a break, she would walk throughout the town asking about opportunities for employment. Each time she returned, she looked up at the window to her room and could clearly see her lovely daughter with her doll at the window.

During the 1920s, a terrible influenza epidemic spread like wildfire throughout the nation, and the town of Loxley did not escape its ravages. Maureen and her beautiful little girl became ill with the dreaded disease. After Maureen had not reported to work for two days, the owner of the hotel went up the stairs to check on her. A terrible sight met him: he found a mother holding her daughter while she rocked her, but there was not a breath of life in either. He arranged for a pauper's funeral, which was more common than not in those terrible times. He had the room cleaned and hired another employee. The new employee soon refused to stay in the room, as the rocking chair would begin to rock at odd times. Guests reported hearing the whimpering sounds of a puppy or perhaps a sick child. However, the most frequent reports of the spirits there came in the form of a little girl seen standing at the upstairs window. She was holding a doll, and her eyes were watching the comings and goings of all who passed on the street.

As long as the hotel was in operation, and even when it was used as private apartments, reports of the haunting of the upstairs room continued. Conductors on the passing train would sometimes point out the hotel to passengers and focus their attention on the upstairs north window. Some would see the girl standing there in the window. Even when the hotel stood vacant, and after the train stopped running, the specter was seen peering toward the tracks. Today, the train tracks and depot are gone, but passersby

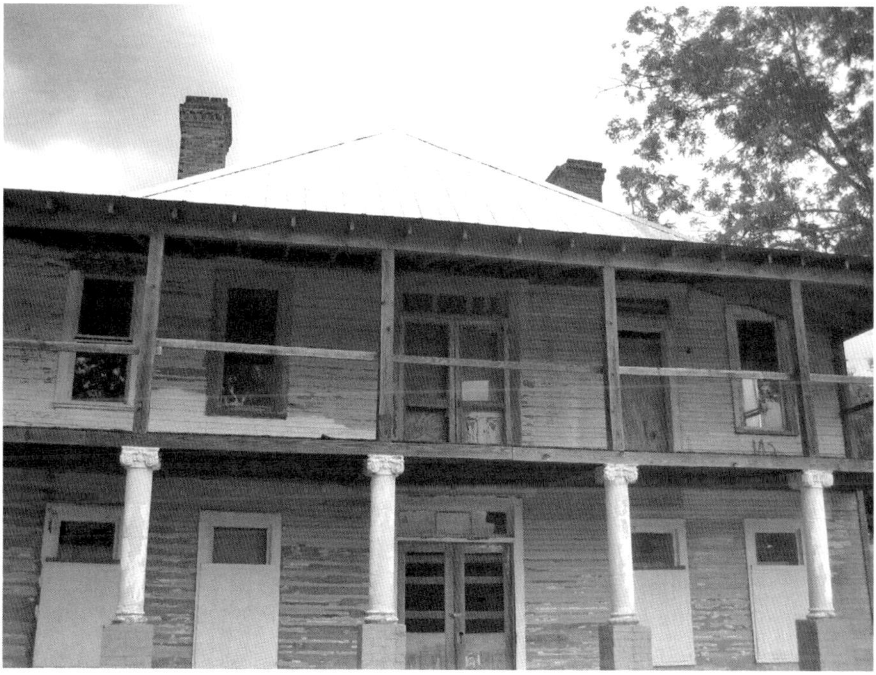

Even with the hotel in a state of disrepair, the little girl is seen in the second-floor right window. *Photo by the author.*

are fascinated by the lovely old building. Some can see the little girl looking down at them. This is the story told often on the front porch of the hotel.

At the time of this publication, the hotel is under new ownership and holds a promising future. The author snapped the photograph of the boarded-up building in 2010. The girl holding her doll is visible in the upstairs window. At the time the hotel sold all of its furnishings, the rocking chair was purchased by a local resident, who has it in her home today. She said that it will start rocking at odd times.

STRING OF PEARLS: FOLEY DEPOT MUSEUM

Pearl turned seventeen on December 7, 1941, the Sunday that the Japanese bombed Pearl Harbor and the United States entered World War II. She lived on the Eastern Shore of Mobile Bay in Daphne. Pearl and Olivia were best friends, having started school together at Daphne in the first grade; they were also classmates at Fairhope High School. During the spring of 1942, all male students who were old enough and qualified left school and headed for the recruitment office. By the time Pearl and Olivia were seniors, most of the young men from their class were serving as active-duty military personnel. Their graduation in 1943 was a bittersweet ceremony. A large poster listing the names of fellow classmen who were serving hung above the stage.

Girls on the homefront certainly did their part. The 4-H club rolled bandages every week for the Red Cross and packed boxes of treats to be mailed to the servicemen overseas. There were many military personnel stationed locally as well. Baldwin County was the temporary home for several units of servicemen. Barin Field in Foley was the aviation training station for the Pensacola Naval Air Station. By April 1944, there were four hundred planes in operation at the base, and the personnel numbered more than 8,000. Fort Morgan was reactivated for World War II home defense, housing Battery F, Fiftieth Coast Artillery Corps, Navy and Coast. There were also two prisoner of war camps in Baldwin County, one in Loxley and one south of Foley off County Road 12 on James Road. The Germans and Italians held there were allowed to work in nearby farms. The Foley camp had as many as 250 prisoners, many creating lasting relationships with the men assigned to guard them, as well as with many local residents.

All of these installations made men in uniform a common sight in Baldwin County, and locals embraced them in every community. A major part of homefront support was the hosting of events at the USO Hall in Foley. The USO was located in the downtown Foley building that had been constructed by the Foley Progressive Club in 1912 for social and cultural events. In 1937, it became American Legion Post No. 99, thus being the logical place to host the weekend programs and dances for sailors and soldiers stationed nearby. This is where Pearl and Olivia spent their weekends.

Each summer, Olivia and her family moved to Foley, where they rented a house near the potato shed they ran there. Pearl stayed in Daphne to work at her family business for most of the week, but on Friday afternoons, she was free to make the trek to Foley for the weekend. Unbeknownst to the army, many a Friday Pearl was able to hitch a ride with the army supply truck that came to Daphne for a pickup before returning to Fort Morgan. The driver, Joey, was homesick for his family and was happy to have some companionship on the bumpy, lonely roads through rural Baldwin County. As two young people are wont to do, Joey and Pearl soon found they had much in common, and both looked forward to the Friday afternoon rides.

Pearl arrived each Friday in Foley, where Joey dropped her off near the potato shed. She and Olivia would run to Olivia's house, share their secrets and make plans for the weekend. Weekend events centered on the USO dances held each Saturday at the hall on Laurel Street in downtown Foley. Olivia lived just a block behind the hall, and the girls were excited each Saturday to decorate the building, bake cakes and make lemonade for the guys who would be bussed in from Barin Field, Fort Morgan and other stations in the area.

After decorating the hall, the girls went home to carefully dress for the evening dance. Pearl usually wore a lovely navy blue dress that she had saved her meager wages to purchase. Since nylon stockings were strictly rationed, the girls took special effort to use their eyebrow pencils to draw seam lines up the backs of their legs. They meticulously used curling irons to crimp their hair in the latest fashion.

Late each Saturday afternoon, the guests would start to arrive at the hall, greeted by many of the locals, who wanted to let them know they were appreciated. Pearl stood behind the punchbowl of lemonade each Saturday night with her eyes darting toward the door until she saw her driver come in. He never knew until the last minute whether he would be able to stay at the dance or not, as he also drove the bus to transport the soldiers, sailors and marines to and fro. When he was able to come in for a while, he had eyes only for Pearl and always walked right up to the lemonade table.

"Would you like some lemonade?" Pearl asked.

"What I would like is a dance," he answered, taking her hand and leading her to the dance floor. The music and night were magic. The Victrola record player was playing a song that soon became their own: "String of Pearls." Glen Miller's big-band sound was the most popular by far. Alabamians felt a special connection with Glen, who had been stationed in Montgomery at Maxwell Air Force Base, and many had heard him in person.

All summer long, the Saturday night USO dances were the stuff that Pearl's dreams were made of. She lived for those dances with her handsome soldier, and he lived for her. Duty called, and he received word that he was to be sent to the European front. On that last Saturday night, when he took her in his arms on the dance floor, the record player once again, as if by some spell, crooned the melody so precious to them. "This will always be our song, and every time I hear it, I will think of us at this time and place, no matter what," he whispered in her ear. He led her outside under the starry sky and gave her a gift: a string of perfectly matched pearls. "Pearls for my Pearl, to pledge my love to you and ask you to be my bride." Pearl did not hesitate, and the two were married the next week.

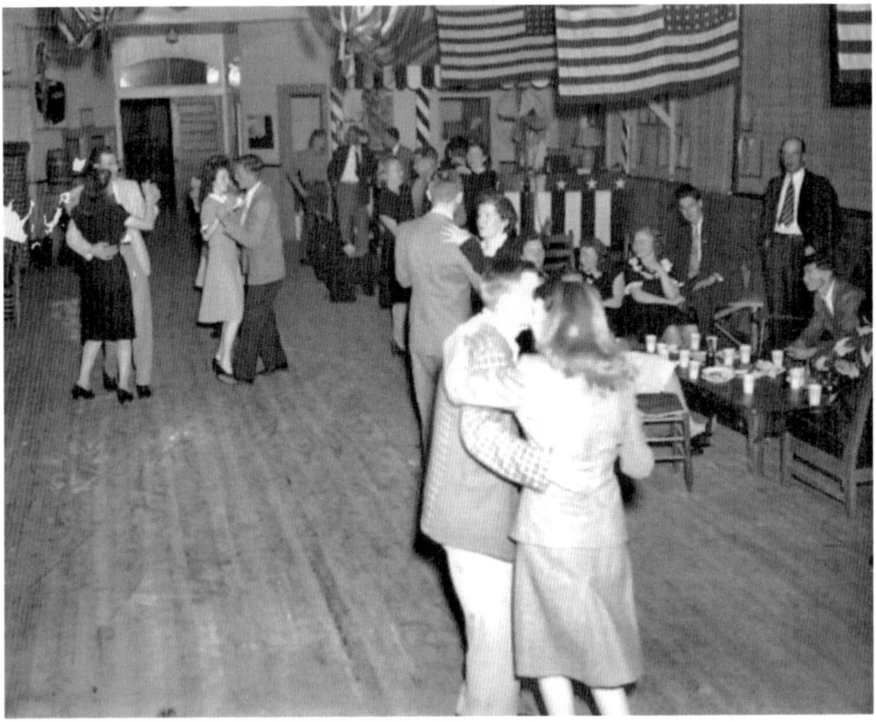

During World War II, USO dances were held at the American Legion Hall, now the Gift Horse Restaurant, Foley. *Courtesy of City of Foley Museum.*

Soon the deployed men were brought to the train depot, where they piled into the passenger cars and crowded at the windows. There the soldiers saw hundreds of citizens lining the tracks for miles, waving American flags, cheering for those men and bidding them Godspeed. Pearl was among those, and as her eyes met Joey's, she touched her precious strand of pearls with one hand and blew a kiss with the other. After he left that day, Pearl never saw him again—at least as far as we know.

She moved to Foley to wait for his return, working in a clothing store downtown. One fateful day, she got the yellow telegram with the dreaded news that her beloved was missing in action. However, her faith in his return never wavered. She often walked the streets wearing her lovely navy blue dress with her string of pearls. People say that she seemed to gradually lose touch with reality and become lost in her own memories. Sometimes she would go into the skating rink that had once housed the USO and glide across the floor, dancing with an unseen partner. In later years, when the building served as a hardware store, she would wander in and ask if anyone would like lemonade. Every evening, at about dusk, she headed toward the depot, where she sat on the bench watching the passengers disembark from the train from Bay Minette.

Pearl continued to live a quiet life, cared for by all the citizens in the town and by Olivia's family, as her own parents had died. She often invited people to the USO dances held each Saturday night to entertain the soldiers stationed in Baldwin County. She told them that her precious driver would be returning soon and that she had to get the lemonade ready for the dance. She had a happy life in her own world. Every day at dusk, she headed to the depot and watched the passengers, knowing that her Joey would be among them.

Pearl died a quiet death and was buried in the pauper's cemetery east of town in an unmarked grave. Residents were saddened and knew that they would miss her walking the streets and sitting on the bench at the depot. Soon after her death, people started reporting that they had seen an ethereal vision walking the streets. She appeared as a mist but resembled a woman in a navy blue dress. Employees in the hardware store, now in the former USO hall, occasionally heard the haunting melody of "String of Pearls." Sometimes one would catch a glimpse of a couple dancing across the floor in the hardware store, seemingly floating on air. Sometimes her image was seen

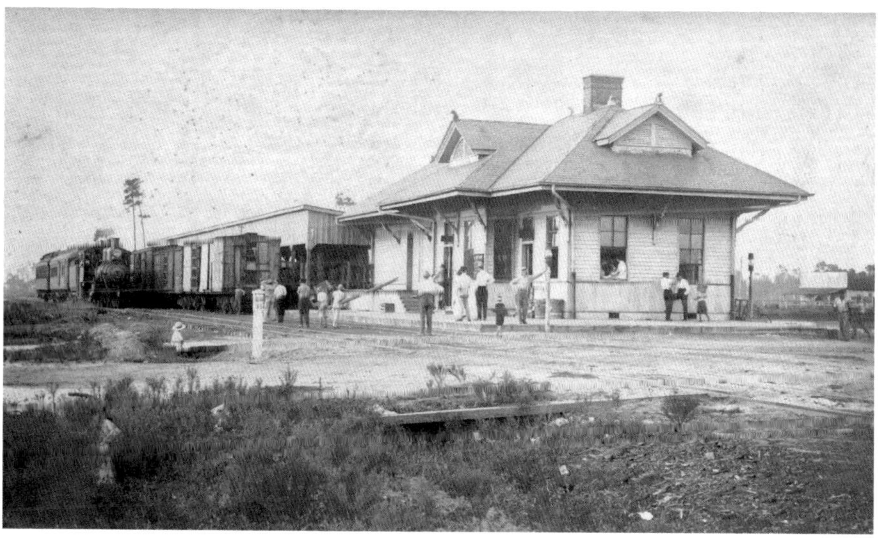

The Foley Depot was the last one on the spur line that ran from Bay Minette daily. This one was built in 1908. *Courtesy of City of Foley Museum.*

sitting on the bench at the defunct and crumbling depot.

The last run of the train for commercial use was in 1971, but the line was used one last time for a bicentennial celebration run using a steam engine. Most passengers were dressed in colonial costumes, but one had on a World War I–era navy blue dress. When the depot was scheduled for demolition, it was rescued by John Snook, owner of Gulf Telephone Company. He moved the building to nearby Magnolia Springs for safekeeping and preserved it until the time came (as he knew it would) when the City of Foley wanted to restore it to its former glory. The building was returned to its original location in 1995 and became the City of Foley Museum. During those twenty-four years of the depot's absence in downtown Foley, no one mentioned seeing the ghostly image. Of course, once the depot was back home, Pearl once again made her presence known to a few fortunate people who had been worried about her. Sometimes at dusk, she was there on the bench facing the tracks—very dim, but a shadow of the past.

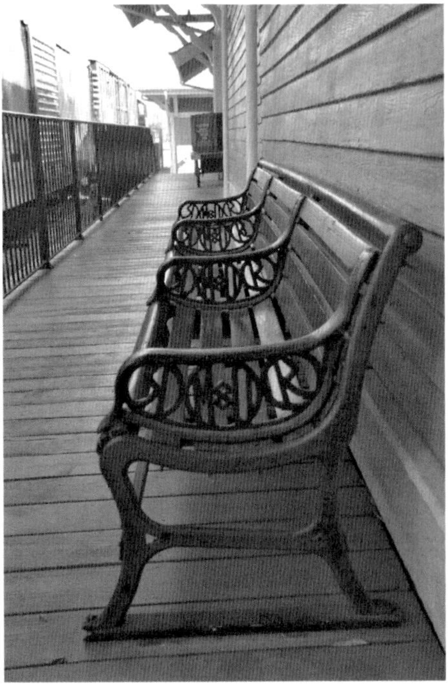

If you are lucky, you will see Pearl sitting on this depot bench late in the evening, waiting for her love to return from the war. *Photo by Penny H. Taylor.*

To this day, at the Gift Horse Restaurant, now in the USO building, once in a while the recorded music seems to take on a life of its own, and the big-band sound of Glen Miller is heard. Diners often ask the server about the handsome couple dancing there among the tables. Those two lovely people: the soldier in a World War II uniform and the girl in a navy blue dress. She is wearing a string of pearls that glows in the dim light. Perhaps you can see them this evening. Would you like a glass of lemonade?

Foley Depot is now open daily as the Foley Train Museum. It houses city artifacts, train memorabilia and a magnificent running model railroad display. www.foleyrailroadmuseum.com.

About the Author

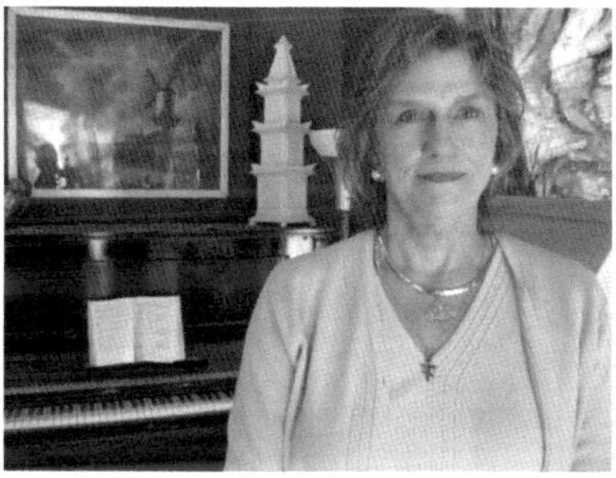

Harriet Brill Outlaw is a retired educator with a deep belief in the preservation of local folklore, and she believes that hauntings in Baldwin County are those spirits pleading for their stories to be told. She has compiled here the best of those stories told on her front porch. She has co-authored three "Images of America" books, produced numerous documentaries on local history and has several media articles to her credit. And she lives with a real ghost!